ATTACKING SOCCER

Jay Miller

Editor

Human Kinetics

Library of Congress Cataloging-in-Publication Data

Miller, Jay, 1948 March 14-
 Attacking soccer / Jay Miller, editor.
     pages cm
1. Soccer--Training. 2. Soccer--Coaching. I. Title.
 GV943.9.T7.M56 2014
 796.334--dc23
                                      2013049710

ISBN: 978-1-4504-2240-6 (print)

Acquisitions Editor: Tom Heine; **Developmental Editor:** Laura Pulliam; **Associate Managing Editor:** Anne E. Mrozek; **Copyeditor:** Alisha Jeddeloh; **Graphic Designer:** Nancy Rasmus; **Graphic Artist:** Kathleen Boudreau-Fuoss; **Cover Designer:** Keith Blomberg; **Photograph (cover):** Fred Kfoury/Icon SMI; **Art Manager:** Kelly Hendren; **Associate Art Manager:** Alan L. Wilborn; **Illustrations:** © Human Kinetics; **Printer:** United Graphics

Printed in the United States of America   10 9 8 7 6 5 4 3 2 1

The paper in this book is certified under a sustainable forestry program.

Human Kinetics

Website: www.HumanKinetics.com

United States: Human Kinetics
P.O. Box 5076
Champaign, IL 61825-5076
800-747-4457
e-mail: humank@hkusa.com

Canada: Human Kinetics
475 Devonshire Road Unit 100
Windsor, ON N8Y 2L5
800-465-7301 (in Canada only)
e-mail: info@hkcanada.com

Europe: Human Kinetics
107 Bradford Road
Stanningley
Leeds LS28 6AT, United Kingdom
+44 (0) 113 255 5665
e-mail: hk@hkeurope.com

Australia: Human Kinetics
57A Price Avenue
Lower Mitcham, South Australia 5062
08 8372 0999
e-mail: info@hkaustralia.com

New Zealand: Human Kinetics
P.O. Box 80
Torrens Park, South Australia 5062
0800 222 062
e-mail: info@hknewzealand.com

E5630

This, my first book, is dedicated
to Curtis Raymond and Ruth Mary Miller
for tackling the task of parenting
the "4 J's" (Joann, John, Jeanne and Jay).
Being the last, I benefited the most.

CONTENTS

DRILL FINDER

Chapter 9   Shooting and Finishing

Chapter 10   Corner Kicks and Throw-Ins

FOREWORD

At a very important time of my career, right after I became the University of Maryland coach, Jay Miller asked me to assist him with the preparation of the U.S. U-17 national team. Those training camps and international tours were vital to my development as a coach. If you have seen Jay coach a team or instruct a coaching course, you have witnessed one of the best soccer voices in the United States. Four things are important for becoming or remaining a top coach: Coach as often as possible, observe or work with the best coaches possible, watch high-quality games, and stay current with the latest coaching methodology. Jay has helped me at all these levels. This book can help you.

Coach Miller and his 11 starting authors take on the task of scoring goals. The Xs and Os of attacking soccer are covered in detail. As a bonus, each coach describes personal experiences on the topic. This book is loaded with excellent training progressions that allow you to create an offense that will break down the opponent's defense. Enjoy reading this book and get your team to score more goals.

Sasho Cirovski
Head Coach, University of Maryland

ACKNOWLEDGMENTS

As hard as I may try, I cannot stop coaching. From the very beginning, I loved the athletic experience. The notion that the whole can be more than the sum of its parts captured me at an early age. This project required me to step up and coach again. As a result of 40 years of trying to cheat the laws of math, I have learned a few things: You need inspiration, you need a plan, and you need to assemble a team. My inspiration to coach was a result of having exceptional coaches. My high school coach Harry Little and my college coach Dr. John McKeon were special. Walter Chyzowych gave me my chance at coaching at the international level, and my experience of coaching with Bob Gansler guided me in the development of a plan, my style of coaching. The quality of the team is everything. I am very proud of my team of 11 authors. Each is very well respected in the coaching community. They all are in demand and very busy, yet without hesitation they offered their time and expertise to this project. I will forever be grateful. Special thanks go to my friend Jeff Pill for his assistance with the early edits.

The staff at Human Kinetics, in particular Tom Heine and Laura Pulliam, have been extremely helpful and patient.

Turnabout is fair play, as I was coached.

Thanks to my wife, Lauren, for the delivery of fresh coffee to my office and a hand on my shoulder to assess my sanity. I love you.

INTRODUCTION

The challenge of offense versus defense continues. As teams develop successful styles of attack, defenses are created and perfected to stop them. This book tackles the task of identifying and honing the skills and tactics necessary for breaking down organized defensive plans.

The team assembled for this book is composed of 11 coaches who have devoted their lives to the craft of coaching and promoting soccer. Their ideas and beliefs have been tested at all levels of competition, resulting in more than 3,500 victories.

The contributors strive to continue developing as coaches, always looking for new and better ways to prepare their teams for the current and future levels of competition. In each chapter, the coaches give personal accounts of how they developed their training sessions. It has been my experience that the best way for coaches to get better is to read past and current publications about coaching methodology and ideas, observe successful coaches in action, discuss ideas of coaching with colleagues, and of course coach as much as possible. For the past 30 years, coaches in the United States have shared training and game-day coaching information with one another. This perplexes professional coaches around the world. Why should they discuss their methods with you? You'll just use those methods to beat them later. Yet American coaches continue to willingly share information for the promotion of soccer. This is an opportunity for you to participate in this sharing of information.

In chapter 1, Jeff Pill, a youth national team coach and U.S. national staff coach, describes activities that emphasize repetition so that players can demonstrate confidence with the ball, which precedes the ability to play with intellect. Jeff is a master at injecting life into any activity. Competition, variety, and enthusiasm cure the boredom of repetition. Jeff offers methodologies for developing a creative environment for learning. The size and shape of the playing grids are specific to each skill level and topic.

In chapter 2, Anson Dorrance demonstrates his philosophy of the training environment for gifted players. The architect of 22 NCAA National Championships has always been able to recruit top-quality players to his program; however, that does not always ensure success. After a disappointing end to a season, Anson concluded that his team's ability to maintain possession was not good enough. Anson started with the standard exercise 5v2 as the cornerstone and developed rigorous competitive exercises where each player's performance is quantified by an objective collection of data. The results showing the pecking order of each player's performance in relationship to the team were displayed daily.

In chapter 3, Tony DiCicco, U.S. women's World Cup champion and Olympic gold medal coach, discusses the role of the goalkeeper in initiating and supporting the team's attack. As a former goalkeeper, national goalkeeper coach, and head coach, Tony outlines activities that address the specialized repetitive skills training for goalkeepers and the inclusion of the goalkeeper in the team's attacking plan. The tactical application of distribution and the use of the goalkeeper as an extra field player to break defensive pressure are featured.

In chapter 4, Mike Noonan, the coach at Clemson, stresses the need to develop the players' soccer intelligence. The role of the modern defender includes the ability to maintain possession and to participate in offensive attacks in the defensive, middle, and final third of the field. The implications of risk and safety for each third are addressed in the training sessions. Mike's sessions test the soccer intelligence of the players under pressure they would experience during an 11v11 competitive game.

In chapter 5, Ken Lolla, national youth coach and the coach at the University of Louisville, is one of best at coaching play in the midfield. His collection of knowledge began as a player in the soccer-rich environment of New Jersey. The teams on which he played and now coach have always displayed the propensity to play and build attacks through the midfield. Attention is given to constant improvement of skill and vision while under pressure through exercises that achieve deep training as described in Daniel Coyle's book *The Talent Code*.

In chapter 6, John Hackworth takes on the topic of creating scoring opportunities in the attacking third. John's extraordinary soccer experiences at the collegiate, international, and now professional levels are evident in the sequence of the training activities. The simple forms of combination play improved by repetition are used to create a variety of ways to attack the defense. Competitive games emphasizing speed create the intensity necessary for developing a team that will attack opponents with confidence and resolve.

In chapter 7, Dean Wurzberger presents a training plan for flank play. Dean's ideas are influenced by his multiple international and domestic coaching licenses and his coaching experience at the U.S. youth national team, collegiate, and professional levels. Dean concentrates on three game situations: flow of the play (central and wide movement of the ball, switch play, counterattacks, and regains), developing overloads (overlaps, underlaps, inside-to-out diagonal runs, and forwards pulling wide), and combination play (movement to receive the ball, dribbling, receiving, turning and playing one touch, wall passes, and rotation). Attention is also given to the passes (crosses) and the timing and location of the runs to receive the passes for an attempt on goal.

In chapter 8, Ian Barker, master coach and NSCAA director of education, presents functional activities to improve the offensive skills of crossing and attacking heading. Ian explains the current trends of attacking influenced by the success of Spain's short passing combination play. However, he points out that a large portion of all goals scored are from crosses and headers. Coach Barker's seven activities characterize the frequency, realism, and progression necessary for improving the functional execution of crossing and finishing.

In chapter 9, Bobby Clark shares his thoughts and methodology on the art and skill of getting the ball into the opponent's goal. Bobby's insight on the development of goal scorers is a result of his storied playing and coaching career. As a player, he competed with and against several of the top scorers in Europe. His coaching career has taken him to New Zealand as men's national coach and to top universities in the United States. His shooting and finishing practices reflect a simple but experienced methodology to the elusive skill of scoring. Take note of his suggestions on pacing the progression: *festina lente*, or hurry slowly.

In chapter 10, Thomas Durkin, former IMG Academy director and coach for the national youth team, MLS, and collegiate levels, applies his considerable experience to the task of diagramming, explaining, and organizing the training of corner kicks and throw-ins. Tom offers information on the design and execution of these restart situations. Take note of the specifics of the timing and angle of the coordinated runs and the timing, spin, and trajectory of the service. In the new world of ultraorganized defenses, the tipping point is often the team with the best restarts.

In chapter 11, Mark Berson, head coach at the University of South Carolina, discusses the organization and details of effective direct and indirect free kicks. In his 30-plus years at USC, Mark has developed a set piece alignment. The alignment consists of three to five tactical options for free kicks taken from all areas in the attacking third of the field. The selection of key players for each free kick is crucial. Extra training time is devoted to the free kick specialists to get the repetitions needed for consistent performance. Coach Berson also explains his philosophy of taking the penalty kick.

KEY TO DIAGRAMS

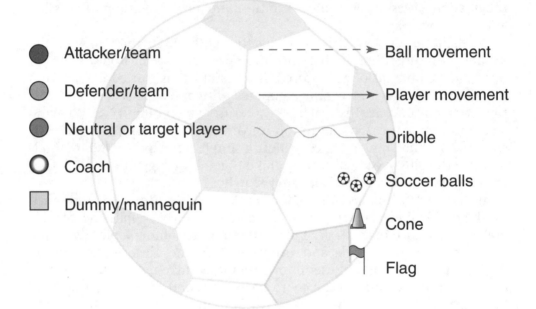

Attacker/team

Defender/team

Neutral or target player

Coach

Dummy/mannequin

Ball movement

Player movement

Dribble

Soccer balls

Cone

Flag

1

Individual Skills: Dribbling, Passing, and Receiving

Jeff Pill

I have several vivid memories of significant soccer experiences growing up. I remember getting my first real, hand-stitched soccer ball that I had to pump up every other day in order to be able to play with it. I remember the first time I was hit in the face with a soccer ball as I tried to block a shot by my friend Ray. Of course, I remember my first goal—a screaming direct kick into the upper right corner.

I also remember being glued to the TV while I listened to Toby Charles and watched *Soccer Made in Germany* on our public television station. What kept me transfixed for the whole game was not the chance to follow a favorite team (although I always liked Bayern Munich, or the *Bayern Munchkins* as we used to call them) but rather watching the amazing skills of the players in front of me. I would eagerly go out to our backyard and try to replicate what I saw. How could they kick the ball effortlessly all the way across the field, and more amazingly, take that pass down with the top of their foot while not missing a step of their overlapping run? How was that guy able to dribble through the tight defense? Bend the ball around a wall? Hit a full-on volley while launching himself in the air? As an eight-year-old, I was mesmerized . . . and hooked. I wanted to be like them!

As I grew up and started playing with older, better players, I realized how challenging it was to get the ball away from a team that was good in possession. As a back, I was always shattered physically and mentally when we had to play teams that were more skillful than we were. Then, playing alongside a bunch of Italians with exquisite skills outside New York City made me realize how much fun it was to play with skilled players. The more my skills improved, the more fun I had. The game seemed to slow down for me as I found that I had more and more time to make decisions. I seemed to have several options available when I had the ball rather than being limited to getting rid of it before someone took it from me.

Now that I am a coach, I realize that the most effective attacking teams are able to place their opponents in situations where they have to choose between two or three threats to their goal at the same time, thereby putting them in a series of catch-22s that eventually lead to conceding a goal.

Even the casual observer recognizes that the more skillful the players are with the ball, the more effective they are in attack and the more entertaining they are to watch. Recent victories by Spain in the 2010 Men's World Cup, Barcelona in the 2011 Champions League, and the Brazilian women's soccer team have emphatically restored faith in the attractive, skillful, attacking soccer that attracts fans across the globe to the beautiful game.

This type of play is not unique to the sport of soccer. How compelling it was to watch Michael Jordan play basketball! I often pitied the poor defenders who were assigned to mark him. They had to choose between coming out to defend his 3-point shot or hanging back to stop his amazing dribble to the basket. Whatever choice they made, they often lost. It is no different when we get to enjoy watching Messi or Marta play. We are often left scratching our heads and saying, "There was nothing that the defender could have done, short of fouling him (or her)!" Messi and Marta teach us that there is still room in the game for the small, skillful player—in fact, that the skillful player is able to rule the game!

Having good technique allows players with the ball to have an impact on the game. While playing, they have the feeling that they are affecting the outcome of the game. What better way for coaches to ensure player retention than helping them develop the tools they need in order to play the game effectively? Teach a person to fish, and he can feed himself for his entire life. Teach a player to play with skill, and she will be able to play for life!

Teaching the skills of the game is all about providing players with a good picture of what the skill looks like and then putting them in environments that replicate the demands of the game and provide quality repetitions. Often, coaches mistake repetitions for development. If that were the case, the best Hacky Sack players would be the best soccer players! But we all know that this is not the case. Players need to be able to apply the skills to gamelike situations where they are under pressure from an opponent, thus being asked to apply their technique to solve a problem.

Of course, small-sided games and training environments will give players the repetition that is needed. Coaches need to remind themselves that the best teacher is a quality game that is appropriate for the developmental stage of the player. When this marriage is perfect, true development takes place.

I have chosen the following environment drills because they are some of my favorites and because they seem to be the players' favorites as well. Most importantly, when used over time, I have found them to have a positive impact on the players' development.

Fundamental-Stage Environment Drills

I have included three fundamental-stage environments that are appropriate during the warm-up phase or during recovery-day training. They allow the players to focus intently on technical execution in a challenging yet unopposed context. In and of themselves, they will not adequately prepare players for the demands they will face in the game, but they serve as a solid building block from which the players perform a high number of repetitions in order to focus on technical precision. In addition, because all three environments are competitive in their structure, the activities often provide the motivation that the players need in order to keep focused and enthused.

Long Passing

Purpose

Improving long passing technique

Organization

Set up two 8- × 8-yard (7 × 7 m) squares 15 to 30 yards (14-27 m) apart. Two teammates are in each square. The more skillful the players, the smaller and farther apart the squares are.

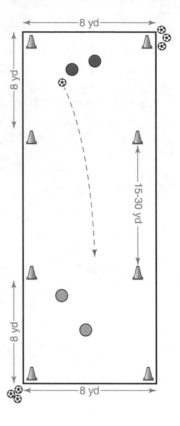

Procedure

1. Play starts when one team kicks the ball into the other team's square.
2. The receiving team must control the ball without letting it go outside the square.
3. Each player is only allowed to play the ball with one touch. A team has three touches in total to play the ball back into the other team's grid.
4. The ball may not stop at any time.
5. Play stops when a shot misses the other team's grid or is not controlled within the grid. Decide beforehand how high a ball may be played to be considered fair.

Key Points

- Use good shooting technique.
- Keep your body balanced, with your weight on your toes.
- Encourage an aggressive shooting mentality.
- Prepare the surface of the body that will receive the ball.
- Drive the ball into the other players' grid to make it difficult to control.
- To receive the ball, get into the line of flight, taking the first touch to prepare the ball for your partner.

Variations

- Work on sending chipped or bent balls into the opponents' grid.
- Make the player's preparing touch go outside the grid so that the serving player has to cross the ball into the opponents' grid. The angle of preparation resembles that of the preparation touch made by someone crossing the ball in the real game.

Central Goal Shooting

Purpose

Learning how and when to shoot; finishing with accuracy

Organization

Set up a 12- × 8-yard (11 × 7 m) area with a central goal designated by flags. Place a pile of extra balls next to the central goal. Form two teams of three, with one player from the defensive team starting in the goal.

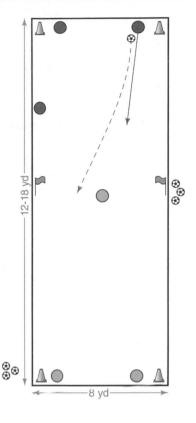

Procedure

1. Play starts when a player from one team shoots the ball from behind the cone off the dribble.

2. After taking the shot, the shooter runs to the goal to become the new keeper.

3. If the original keeper makes the save, he quickly turns and passes the ball to a teammate waiting behind the cone, who in turn shoots as quickly and accurately as possible. If the original keeper does not make a save, he gets the nearest ball and puts it into play. This ball may be the one coming through the goal or one from the pile of extra balls next to the central goal. In any case, the ball must come from the returning keeper before a shot is taken.

4. Immediately after the ball is put into play, the shooter becomes the new keeper. The activity is ongoing to allow quality repetitions in a short amount of time. Players must go from offense to defense quickly.

Key Points

- Watch for players backing up or moving to the side before they shoot. Players should shoot with a fluid motion and follow through toward the target.

- Strike the ball on the top half in order to keep the ball low and toward the goal.

- Use various surfaces of the foot in order to put a variety of spins on the ball.

Variations

- Players shoot off a dribble.
- Players shoot a first-time ball that is played from the returning keeper.
- Players shoot a first-time ball that is played from a teammate who is waiting behind the cone with them.
- Players shoot a volley out of the air served from the returning keeper.

2v2 Heading Competition

Purpose

Playing balls in the air; heading

Organization

Set up 8-yard (7 m) goals 10 yards (9 m) apart. Form two teams of two players each where the defending team is positioned in its goal area and the attacking team starts play from its half of the field.

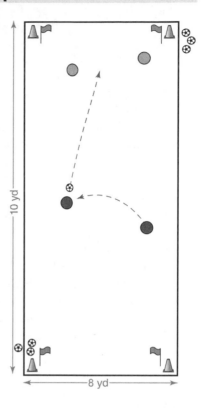

Procedure

1. Play starts with an attacking player tossing the ball to a teammate's head.
2. Once the ball leaves the hand, only the head can be used by either player.
3. The attacking team attempts to score over the line by heading the ball past defenders.
4. The ball must pass below the shoulders to count as a goal.
5. Defenders can make saves with their hands.
6. Attackers can head the ball back and forth as many times as they would like before they take a shot.

Key Points

- Use good heading technique.
- Run into good attacking angles.
- Counterattack quickly after a save is made.

Variations

- Allow the attackers to first serve the ball to themselves.
- Require players to make at least two or more headers before attacking the goal.
- Defending players may not use their hands to save an attempt on goal.

Opposed Environments

To ensure development, players must progress past these fundamental environments into opposed training activities. It is one thing for players to be highly technical. It is certainly another, more important thing for them to be able to apply their technical competencies to the actual game environment. Applied technique is much more essential than isolated technique. Thus, this second section of activities challenges players to apply their technique when they are under the pressure from an opponent. Now they must make decisions regarding how, when, where, and why they apply their technique.

The opposed environments are structured in such a way as to ensure ample focused repetitions while at the same time providing the realism that is essential for game success. The three warm-up games described earlier can be used for any session that focuses on finishing. Players are asked to drive balls over distance and head or shoot on goal, all essential technical proficiencies of finishing. Thus, these activities can be appropriately followed by Flying Changes, Bread and Butter, and Two-Zone Shooting, which are described in this section. In this case, it is better to not use the same sequence each time the games are played. This keeps player interest higher and thus enhances motivation. The End Zone game is a good intermediate activity, perhaps best used after the warm-up and before the team plays to goal. It emphasizes possession, player roles, and team shape, and it is a great transition to Bread and Butter or Two-Zone Shooting. In any case, it is up to each coach's individual artistry to put these environments together in such a way that they come alive for the players and lead them along the road to improving their technical competencies.

Bread and Butter

Purpose

Improving finishing technique and skill

Organization

On half of a standard field, set up an area that is 40 yards (37 m) long and the width of the standard field. Set up 10- × 10-yard (9 × 9 m) corner boxes at each corner and a portable goal on the end line opposite the regular goal. There are

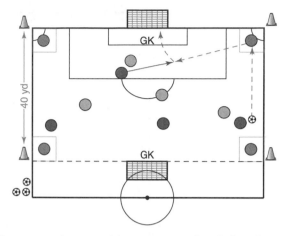

three teams of four and two goalkeepers. An attacking team and a defending team position in the main area, and the players of the third team position inside the corner boxes and are neutral, supporting either the attacking or defending teams.

Procedure

1. Play starts when one team attacks the other in the main area.
2. If the attacking players score, they then quickly retrieve a ball out of their own goal and attack again. At this time the defending players leave the field and take the place of the team in the corner boxes.
3. Play resumes as described previously. Supporting players can move inside their square but are limited to two touches on the ball. They can come onto the playing field and even shoot if possible.

Key Points

- After scoring a goal, the attacking players should look to play quickly before the other team has a chance to come on and get organized.
- Find the best penetration option. This may mean using the target player on the end line, dribbling, shooting, or finding the highest attacking player with a pass. If there are no penetration options, the emphasis switches to possession. Find a player who is able to penetrate.
- Use attacking and defending principles of play.
- Use accurate shooting.
- Create scoring chances with ball movement and timing of runs.
- Goalkeepers should use good technique.

Variation

Play a regular 5v5 game without corner players.

Flying Changes

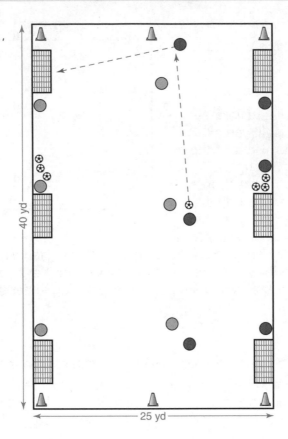

Purpose

Improving passing skills and tactics

Organization

Set up an area that is 40 × 25 yards (37 × 23 m), placing three small training goals on each end line and cones to designate a midfield line. There are two teams of six players each. Three players from each team are on the field at a time while the remaining three players wait on their own end line.

Procedure

1. Play starts with one team attacking the other.
2. If the ball leaves a team's half of the field because of a shot, incomplete pass, tackle, or so on, the team members leave the field and are replaced by the waiting three players from their team. Only the three players in whose half the ball went out leave the field; the other three opponents stay and try to absorb the counterattack. It does not matter who plays the ball out of bounds or scores the goal; as soon as the ball leaves your half of the field, you leave the field.

3. The new players waiting on the end line come on right away and try to quickly counterattack.

Key Points

- Attacking players should find the free player and the free goal.
- Attacking players should counterattack quickly.
- Attacking players should execute proper tactical decisions regarding when to dribble, pass, or shoot.
- Defenders should recover and defend after their team loses the ball if they remain on the field.
- If the ball is not under pressure, drop immediately as a team and defend the three goals.
- Once the goals are safe, the defending team attempts to put the ball under pressure. This is done by anticipating passes and stepping up to defend when the ball is rolling between attackers or allowing the attackers to dribble into pressure.

Variations

- Play with gates instead of goals and allow 3 points if a player is able to dribble through the gate.
- Play 4v4.
- Play with a full-time central attacking player (forward).
- Play with a full-sized goal in the middle, defended by a keeper. Goals in this central goal count for 3 points, while goals scored in the wide goals count for 1 point. Play up to 10 points for each round.

End Zone

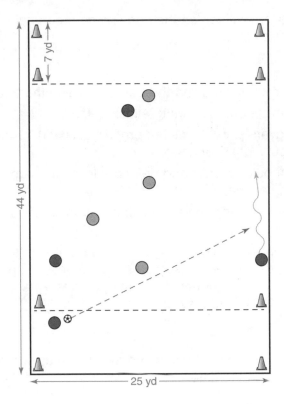

Purpose

Improving passing skills and tactics

Organization

Set up an area that is 44 × 25 yards (40 × 23 m) with a 7-yard (6 m) end zone at each end. The field must be large enough to allow opportunities to dribble and pass but small enough that dribbling players must make decisions about when to dribble and pass. There are two teams of four or five players each.

Procedure

1. Play starts with the coach tossing the ball into the center area for either team to gain possession. After this, play restarts as a regular game. The coach may decide to use throw-ins or kick-ins when the ball leaves the field of play or when a goal is scored.

2. Teams attempt to get the ball into the opponents' end zone by passing or dribbling.

3. Teams may play the ball back into their own end zone without it being defended in that zone (it is a free zone).

Key Points

- Use proper dribbling, passing, and receiving mechanics.
- Make proper dribbling and passing decisions.

Variations

- Add goals and a keeper for each team.
- Remove the end zone.
- Play with a neutral player who plays in attack for both teams.
- Restrict players to only being able to pass into the zone or only being able to dribble into the zone.
- Place a restriction on the pass so that it can only count as a goal if the receiving player was not already in the end zone when the pass was made (the receiving player must run into the end zone after the pass is made).

Two-Zone Shooting

Purpose

Improving long-range shooting and creating finishing chances

Organization

Double the penalty box for the playing area with goals at each end. There are two teams of four players each and two goalkeepers.

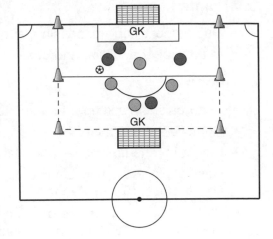

Procedure

1. Play starts with the coach giving possession to one team. After this, play is always started by the keeper of the team in possession. If a team scores a goal, it keeps possession. There are no throw-ins or corner kicks.

2. Each team has three players in its defensive half and one player in the attacking half. Players are restricted to their own half.

3. If the one player in the attacking half scores a goal, it is worth double points. This encourages the player to work hard to win the ball and to look for rebound opportunities.

Key Points

- Use good team shape (wide players get wide to make it difficult for the one player to defend).
- Keep the ball moving in possession.
- Look to play the ball into the attacker in the attacking half if possible.

Variations

- Play with more or fewer players.
- Allow one attacker to move into the attacking half from the back once the ball is played in.

2

Team Possession

Anson Dorrance

The University of North Carolina women's soccer program is the most successful soccer program in NCAA (National Collegiate Athletic Association) history. Although there are constants to the program's success, the reality of the UNC women's soccer team is that achievement is gained through a constant desire to improve and a willingness to use the successful ideas that are all around us to try to keep the team on the cutting edge.

In 2011, my North Carolina Tar Heels were eliminated in penalty kicks by the well-coached and gritty University of Central Florida (UCF) Knights in the third round of the NCAA tournament. With every afternoon for the remainder of the fall now free, I was afforded the opportunity to study what our excellent men's team was doing in its training environments. Carlos Somoano, a longtime assistant for the newly departed Elmar Bolowich, was our men's first-year head coach. Watching his team all fall had been valuable for me and very enjoyable. I have always felt that the evolution of the women's game would be faster if we used the men's game as our model, and watching the team that would soon become the 2011 men's collegiate national champions was inspiring. Now it was time for me to study them in training, and fresh off a disappointing end to our season, I knew I could learn something.

What struck me immediately was that our men started every training session with 5v2 in a 10- × 10-yard (9 × 9 m) grid one touch, with an objective of completing at least 20 passes before being dispossessed. In their 5v2, the ball could leave the grid as long as the players continued one touch and got the ball back into the grid as quickly as possible. The speed and urgency of play was incredible! In our loss to UCF at the NCAA tournament, our team passing percentage was an abysmal 51 percent. The entire season we were hovering around 54 percent. It was obvious we needed to increase our ability to possess the ball, and what I was observing with the men's team clearly addressed that. Also, their 5v2s did not begin when practice began; they began when there was a critical mass of seven players.

I wasted no time in stealing this approach, and every one of my sessions in the spring of 2012 began with 5v2s. We took our old get-reacquainted time at the start of practice and threw a ball into it. It was still informal and social, but now it was with a ball—the players were passing, and it was not easy to play this 5v2. One touch in a 10 × 10 grid, especially if the defenders turn up the heat, is a significant challenge. Of course, 20 passes for us was near impossible, but Carlos convinced me to stay with that as a goal and to stay with one touch. Additionally, any nick by a defender would trade out the defender who nicked it. These details pushed our players. Because our 5v2s began like the men's, when seven players arrived, we maximized our time to complete passes in training, and those who showed up first got more passes in. I loved the entire concept, but we weren't finished tinkering.

While our 2011 men's team was steaming toward the national championship that fall, Swansea City was making a successful transition from the championship into the English Premier League (EPL). What shocked all of us who followed the EPL was how well Swansea coach Brendan Rodgers' boys could keep the ball, even against the best teams in the league, and how comfortably they cleared relegation in the first year after promotion. I picked up on a rumor that Rodgers tried to get 2,000 passes in every Swansea training session. Whether he did or not, it was clear how good they were in possession, and I liked the idea of jacking up the number of passes in every practice. With the aid of my newly appointed match and performance analyst Jason Sisneros, we created a system for ranking players based on possession in training and increasing the number of passes per session.

Clearly the platform for 2,000 passes has to evolve beyond a simple 5v2. Using Rodgers' 2,000 passes as a new ideal, along with several training concepts stolen from our men's team, we embarked on a new plan of possession in the UNC women's soccer program. What I have selected to share here are the passing environments we ended up fine-tuning over the course of our 2012 national championship season. Although many factors are involved in any team's success, what was clear from our match data in 2011, where our passing percentage lingered around 54 percent, and our 2012 season, where we routinely completed over 60 percent of our passes as a team, was that our focus on improved possession made a difference for us, and these exercises worked.

Here are a few things we did in training that made a difference for us:

- Increased overall team ability to retain possession.
- Improved individual ability to keep possession in passing.
- Identified and categorized players based on their possession abilities.
- Drove this structure through competition and measured results.

Player Performance Matrix

To drive performance, Jason Sisneros and I dedicated our efforts to creating a system of simple yet substantive rankings so that our players would be driven into deep practice. Our most refined system is the 5v2 matrix, a system of promotion and relegation where we track passes in the 5v2 and calculate a score for each player's performance that day.

The following table shows one day of 5v2 at the University of North Carolina:

Today's rank	Player	Passes completed	Times in	Average pass completion	5v2 score
1	Brigman	24	0	24	58
2	Elby	35	2	17.5	52.5
3	McFarlane	26	1	26	52
4	Dunn	29	2	14.5	43.5
5	Nigro	32	3	10.7	42.7
6	Ohai	28	3	9.3	37.3
7	Parker	26	4	6.5	32.5
8	Lindquist	16	1	16	32
9	Bruce	23	3	7.7	30.7
10	Harris	22	3	7.3	29.3
11	Williamson	21	4	5.25	26.7
12	Bowen	18	3	6	24
13	Clay	19	4	4.75	23.8
14	Neilsen	17	3	5.7	22.7
15	Ramirez	18	4	4.5	22.5
16	Gardner	18	4	4.5	22.5
17	Green	12	3	4	16
18	Murray	12	6	2	14
19	Haeberlin	10	4	2.5	12.5
20	Sieloff	8	3	2.7	10.7
21	Ball	8	4	2	10
		Total passes completed	Total times in	Team completion average	Team 5v2 score
		422 (20.1 player average)	64 (3 player average)	6.6	26.7

> continued

Our 5v2 matrix tracks completed and incomplete passes, calculates a pass ratio, and determines each player's performance in the form of a score. The 5v2 score is a calculation of a player's pass ratio plus total passes completed. In this way, we value players who make fewer mistakes while completing more passes, and everything is based on an average. Our matrix calculates team averages and scores the team for the day as well.

Players are grouped according to those who did equal to or better than both team averages, those who perform equal to or better than one of the two team averages, and those who did not meet or exceed either. Our players are aware of where they stand. Every time we play, everyone else is aware of where their teammates stand because we publicly announce the divisions and split off into those groups during our possession trainings. This puts a positive pressure on the individuals to succeed and creates an environment where the details matter and performance improves over time.

The element that I think drives the players to concentrate the most is the pressure of promotion and relegation. The top two players in the 5v2 are promoted and the bottom two are relegated, so every day there is a positive gamelike stress on every player to focus.

5v2 Divisions

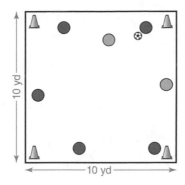

Purpose

Identifying top 5v2 players and potential playmakers

Organization

Set up a 10- × 10-yard (9 × 9 m) grid. There are seven total players, with five attackers and two defenders.

Procedure

1. Designate two players to start as defenders in the middle. The five attackers start with the ball on the coach's whistle.
2. Players play one touch at 100 percent speed for three 90- to 120-second games, with 60 seconds active rest between games where all players focus on rolling accurate, properly paced passes and receiving the ball with open body positions.
3. If defense gets a touch, the defender who's been in the longest and the attacker who played a poor pass trade.

Key Points

- Passes must be crisp, firm, and rolling on the ground.
- Short support is critical with an open body position to receive and play quickly.
- Third attackers are always showing and moving in the windows between defenders for a split pass.

5v2 Parlow Transition

Purpose

Playing 5v2 with transition between offense and defense and possession elements of the 5v2, with defenders retaining possession if they win the ball

Organization

Set up two connected 10- × 10-yard (9 × 9 m) or 12- × 12-yard (11 × 11 m) grids. There are 12 players, with 5v2 in grid A and 4v1 in grid B.

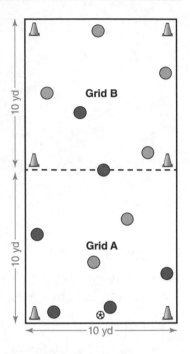

Procedure

1. Play starts in the 5v2 grid.
2. In their attacking grid, players must complete 5 to 10 passes for a goal.
3. Defenders must win the ball and play a successful pass to their attacking grid (grid B) to score. If the ball is lost on offense (grid A) and the defending team plays a successful pass to its attacking grid (grid B), transition occurs and one attacker and one defender sprint into grid B to join the lone defender to create the 5v2 scenario.
4. Repeat this process as each team has possession, loses possession, or transitions between each phase as the game continues.

Key Points

- Vision and anticipation are crucial.
- There is no touch restriction.

3v3+1 Playmaker

Purpose

Developing playmakers

Organization

Set up a 20- × 30-yard (18 × 27 m) grid. There are two teams of three players each and an additional playmaker (full-time offense).

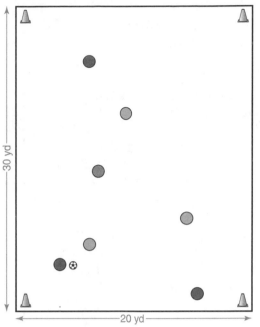

Procedure

Play starts with one team in possession. There are three ways to play this game:

1. The playmaker has one touch and everyone else has two; five passes are worth one goal.

2. The emphasis is not to show the ball to the defender under pressure, shield it, or spin it away from pressure.

3. Allow unlimited touch, with every successful wall pass worth one goal and five passes worth one goal so that the emphasis is on combining.

Key Points

- The playmaker must stay fully engaged and active.
- The playmaker must create a good angle of support and angles to play into.

Final-Pass End-Zone Game

Purpose

Combining possession, transition, penetration, and finishing

Organization

Set up an area that is 60 × 65 yards (55 × 59 m) with a 15-yard (14 m) midfield zone and a 7-yard (6 m) final pass zone on each end next to the midfield zone. There are two teams of seven players each plus three playmakers. Six players from each team and the playmakers position in the midfield zone and one player from each team acts as a goalkeeper in each goal. Formation is one goalkeeper, three defenders, two wide players, and one target forward, with three playmakers (full-time offense) underneath the target forward.

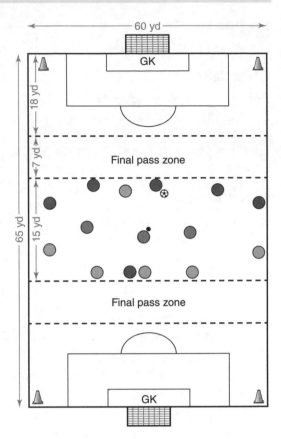

Procedure

1. Play starts with the ball played into the field for one team to gain possession.

2. Possession is restricted to the midfield zone until a final entry pass is made and received in the 7-yard (6 m) final pass zone.

3. The receiving player must take at least one touch in the final pass zone; then she is in on goal.

4. The receiving player has a maximum of three touches (one to receive plus two) to either finish or lay off a pass or cross for a one-touch finish from supporting attackers.

5. When in one goal, the receiving player may be joined by unlimited additional attackers. No defenders may enter. (Once a team has achieved a high enough level of play, defenders may transition into the attacking zone.)

6. For better game flow, let every play finish, even if a player is offside or if a ball is not received in the final zone.

Key Points

- Use proper accuracy and pace of passes.
- Use angles of support and vision to look for penetrating balls into the final pass zone.
- Selection of the correct seam to play the ball is crucial. Timing and angles of runs are also crucial.
- Composure around and inside the box
- This game can be scored several ways based on ball entry into the final zone, ball entry beyond the final zone, combinations used to get into the final zone, and so on.

3

Goalkeeper in the Attack

Tony DiCicco

In the modern game of world soccer, the role of the goalkeeper continues to expand. Clearly, the goalkeeper's number one job is still to be the last defender, the organizer of the defense, the player who is expected to solve the breakdowns and prevent the team from suffering goals. However, much more is expected from the goalkeeper, including the ability to have a positive offensive impact for the team.

These offensive skills include the ability to distribute with the hands quickly, accurately, and over distance. Top keepers make a save and quickly distribute to a teammate to begin a counterattack. To understand how critical a keeper's attacking role can be one only has to remember Tim Howard's distribution for the United States in the final 2010 World Cup group game versus Algeria that ended with Landon Donovan's historic goal, sending the United States into the knockout round as group winner.

Hand distribution includes sling throws over distance, bowl rolls along the ground, and baseball sidearm throws that lead streaking players and allow them to easily collect and run with the ball. Possession is so vital in the modern game that training these techniques is critical. The training must include game situations requiring the goalkeeper to make the right decisions regarding what throw to use, where to throw the ball in relationship to the defense, and who to connect with.

The goalkeeper's ability to distribute with the feet is as important as hand distribution. For high-level keepers, the ratio of playing with feet versus hands is approximately 10 to 1. These skills include long and accurate goal kicks; punts, dropkicks, and the popular side volley kicks; and of course the ability to receive balls, make good player decisions, and connect passes in and around the keeper's defensive third or, when needed, upfield.

Are we fully training, improving, and utilizing the attacking abilities of the goalkeeper? Against a high-pressuring team playing with a three-front, can we maintain possession by using our keeper as an additional field player and outlet, or does the pressure force our team out of our possession game plan? If we are playing against a high-pressuring team, can we lure opponents closer to our goal and then create a counterattacking opportunity with a long, accurate, direct ball from our keeper? Can our team play a higher defensive restraining line because our keeper is trained and confident to read through balls, come out and cover the space and win balls behind our backs and outside the penalty area with her feet, and make good distribution decisions? With a confident keeper who has foot skills, our team may be able to play a variety of systems such as 1-3-4-3 or 1-3-5-2 or play a higher defensive restraining line to condense the attack. As coaches, we need to create the environment and then emphasize our keeper's attacking potential. To help take your keeper to the next level of attacking soccer, your training should meet the following criteria:

- Goalkeeper–coach training—This means one on one or the goalkeeper coach with three or four keepers.
- Goalkeeper–coach–players training—This uses a group of players and a coach to train the keeper.
- Goalkeeper–coach–team training—This uses the entire team and a coach to train the keeper.

Goalkeeper Distribution One-Touch Shot

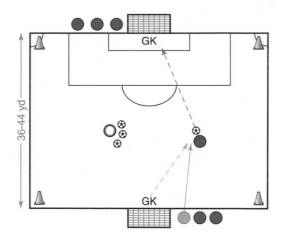

Purpose

Improving the goalkeeper's ability to distribute with the hands

Organization

Set up an area on half of a standard field with the main goal on one end line and a portable goal 36 to 44 yards (33-40 m) away, depending on the keepers' level. There are at least six shooters (three positioned next to each goal) and two goalkeepers. Place a supply of balls in the center of the training area next to the coach.

Procedure

1. Play starts when the first shooter in line moves into the playing area to shoot a ball that is fed by the coach.

2. The keeper makes the save and then distributes using a bowl roll to the first shooter in the opposite line, who is streaking forward and has to shoot on the first touch. The bowl must be accurate, correctly paced, and simple to run onto and strike.

3. If the other keeper makes the save from this shooter, then he distributes using the bowl technique to the next shooter in the other line and the exercise continues in this manner.

4. If the shot misses the goal or is scored, the coach plays a ball to the goalkeeper to field with his hands and distribute to the next shooter.

Key Points

- Use proper saving techniques and decisions.
- Use proper bowling technique. Underhand roll to a teammate who is relatively close (less than 20 yd or 18 m). The ball should not bounce but should instead resemble a good short foot pass.

Variation

Determine the distance between goals based on the age and ability of the players. The older and more developed they are, the farther apart the goals may be.

Goalkeeper Distribution Wide From a Saved Shot

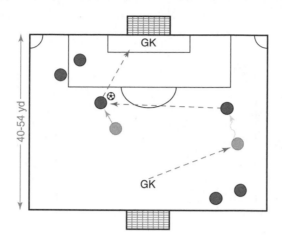

Purpose

Improving the goalkeeper's ability to distribute with the hands after saving a shot on goal

Organization

Set up an area with goals that are 40 to 54 yards (37-49 m) apart, depending on the keepers' level. There are six players plus two goalkeepers. Two players are positioned wide and to the right of each goal (outside backs or wide midfielders) and two players are positioned in the center of the field (forwards). Place a supply of balls in the center of the field.

Procedure

1. One player shoots on a keeper and when the save is made, a wide player makes a bent run wide and upfield at speed.
2. Using a baseball sidearm or sling sidearm throw, the keeper leads the sprinting player into space so that she can take one touch and serve it into the penalty area for the next shooter.
3. If the keeper saves the ball, the same thing happens on the weak (opposite) side.
4. If the ball is errant or a goal is scored, the exercise restarts from the shooters out front.
5. After the cross, the wide player circulates behind the goal to the other side.
6. The exercise is continuous.

Key Points

- Use proper saving techniques and decisions.
- Use proper throwing technique.

Goalkeeper Distribution Wide After a Cross or Shot

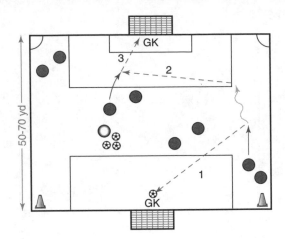

Purpose

Improving the goalkeeper's ability to distribute with hands after saving a shot or catching a cross.

Organization

Set up an area on half of a standard field with the main goal on one end line and a portable goal 50 to 70 yards (46-64 m) away, depending on the keepers' level. There are eight players plus two goalkeepers. Two shooters are at the top of the 18-yard (16 m) box for each goal. Two wide players are positioned wide and to the right of each goal. Place a supply of balls in the center of the field.

Procedure

1. Play starts with a player shooting the ball and a goalkeeper making the save.

2. The keeper takes a few quick steps and launches a strong sling throw to the opposite flank to a wide player, who receives the pass and crosses it into the penalty area for the keeper to handle the situation against two attackers. The attackers should shoot or head the ball at goal using one touch. The exercise continues with the keeper distribution pass to the opposite side.

3. If the cross is errant, the exercise restarts with a shot from outside the 18-yard (16 m) box.

4. The exercise is continuous.

Key Points

- Putting keepers in this environment while saving a shot or handling a cross gives them a chance to perform repetitions of their throwing techniques in a gamelike scenario. The field players start to read the keeper's response after a save. They also are training their skills of finishing, crossing, running with the ball, and so on.

- The keeper should almost always look to the weak side for distribution. Switch the direction of the exercise so as to train both sides.

- This type of training exercise works best before or after training when the goalkeeper coach and some players can make the environment for the keepers more realistic.

Goalkeeper Possession in the Defensive Third

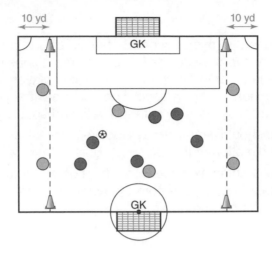

Purpose

Training the goalkeeper to improve foot skills and contribute to possession in the defensive third

Organization

Set up a half-field area for senior-level keepers (shorter length for junior players and keepers). On each flank, create lanes that are 10 yards (9 m) wide for the support players. One team plays with six players on the field. The other team plays with two players on the field, four players in the support lanes, and two keepers. Place a supply of balls in each goal.

Procedure

1. Play starts by giving possession to the team with six players in the center area of the field. They can score on either goal whenever they win the ball. They should be able to create a shot on goal almost every time.

2. The other team can only possess the ball. They possess the ball using the two keepers and the four wide players to prevent the other team from getting the ball. The wide players may only use two touches.

3. The game is played for 6 minutes, and every 2 minutes, the two center players change. After 6 minutes, the role of each team changes. The team with the most goals at the end of the 12-minute match wins.

Note that keepers must work to alleviate pressure and keep possession. If the keeper can't possess the ball, he looks to play a long ball to the opposite keeper. This long ball from keeper to keeper can be caught (rather than played like a back pass) and then distribution starts again. Don't let wide players play to the wide players; they have to play back into the game to their two teammates or to the keepers. When the ball goes out of play or a goal is scored, play resumes with the keeper using a hand serve. Use these rules as a guide and adjust them to meet the specific needs of your keeper and team.

Key Points

- Evaluate the keepers' support positions, ability to receive a ball, and ability to find an open option to maintain possession. There will likely be some technical mistakes in receiving as well as distribution.
- Evaluate the keepers' ability to recognize when it does not make sense to possess the ball and it is better tactically to play long and out of danger (to the opposite keeper).

Variation

Adjust the rules if needed to make sure the keepers play a big role in possession so that they will improve their foot skills and distribution decisions.

Goalkeeper Commanding the Space
Behind the Defense

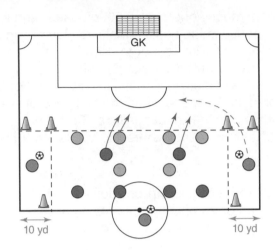

Purpose

Improving the goalkeeper's ability to organize and control the space behind the defense

Organization

Set up a half-field area. The exercise starts in an area 35 yards (32 m) from goal to the midfield line. Mark two service areas that are 10 yards (9 m) wide on each flank plus a central service area just over midfield. There are six players on each team in the central area. There is a neutral player in each of the three service areas. The keeper is in the goal area.

Procedure

1. Play starts with one team in possession trying to play a ball over the 35-yard (32 m) line to a teammate for an attempt on goal. The pass may be played from any of the 6+3 players in possession. Offensive or defensive players may not enter the space behind the 35-yard (32 m) line until the pass is made.

2. Various types of passes may come from any of the three service areas, such as balls played over the top, balls played through the gaps, balls bent behind the defense, or straight balls played toward the goal from servers 2 or 3. The passes into the attacking third need to force decisions from the keeper and should not be played so that the field players always get the first touch.

3. When the keeper calls for the ball, the strikers can try to score but must avoid all contact. This is important so that the keeper knows she will not be tackled or run into even if she makes a bad decision; of course, this also prevents injuries during training. Also, the coach needs to identify and define the communication requirements and options for the keeper and the defensive players.

Key Points

- This is a tactical exercise that will challenge the keeper's decision making, technical ability to clear the ball, and ability to deal with breakaway situations.
- One of the key components of this exercise is identifying the communication requirements of the keeper.

Variations

- Move the restraining line and servers closer to the goal. This will adjust the keeper's starting position.
- Players, including the servers, can shoot directly at goal if the keeper's position is too extended. Ideally, the keeper is in a position where he feels he can get back to his goal line if a shot is taken. However, his body language and momentum are ready to go forward to win the through ball in the penalty area with sound breakaway technique or outside the penalty area with foot skills.
- Organize 4v4+2 in the central area with a neutral player in the service areas on both flanks so you have three groups of four that will rotate. Teams try to possess the ball long enough to put a teammate through onto goal. The offside line is the grid line closest to the goal; any player receiving a ball to go to goal must have been in the grid or on the line when the ball was played. Any attacking player, including the plus players or the servers, can play a player through so that the keeper must deal with the through ball or the breakaway situation. Allow any attacking players, including the servers, to shoot (chip the keeper) if the keeper is too extended from the goal line. Start with the defenders not being able to chase in the attacking player and then phase into allowing one attacker and one defender to join the first attacker after the through ball is played. When the ball is dead, always restart from a server on the side.

Goalkeeper Building From the Back

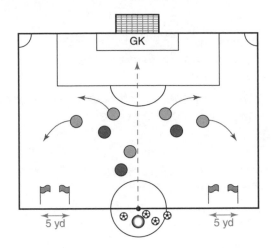

Purpose

Improving a team's ability to create an attack started by the keeper in possession of the ball

Organization

Set up a half-field area. Using flags, place two goals that are 5 yards (5 m) wide on the flank areas of the midfield line. There is one team of five players plus a goalkeeper (the five include the four backs and one holding midfielder) and another team of three players.

Procedure

Phase 1

1. Play starts with one of the coaches playing a ball to the keeper.
2. The keeper collects and distributes the ball to either a wide defender or a central defender.
3. From there the team uses the keeper as needed to possess the ball against the other team, finishing with a goal through the cone goals at midfield in the channels.
4. Whenever the defending team wins the ball, it must play back to the keeper to force possession and decisions from the keeper.

Phase 2

1. Add another defender and a target player at midfield, which will require more keeper play and more decisions by the keeper. (The exercise is now five plus the goalkeeper and the target versus four.)

2. If possession is too much of a risk, the keeper plays long to the target, who then plays to a blue supporting player, who resumes the attack.

3. Whenever the defending team wins the ball, it must play back to the keeper to force possession and decisions from the keeper.

Phase 3

1. Add two more midfield players on the defending team and one midfielder on the other (six plus the goalkeeper and the target versus five). In this organization it may be wise to release one of the midfielders to an advanced position in the midfield and draw a defender along.

2. If the defender stays, then the midfielder is a direct option that the keeper needs to consider. If the defender goes with the midfielder, the numbers in the back for possession become more manageable.

Key Points

- When the keeper is about to win the ball, the outside backs clear high and wide with bent runs.
- The center backs split and the holding midfielder occupies the central area.
- Focus on the keeper's distribution technique and decision making.

Counterattacking From the Goalkeeper

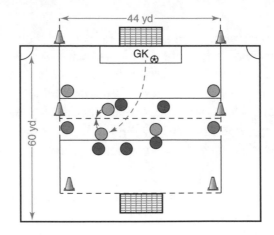

Purpose

Improving a team's ability to start a counterattack quickly from its defensive half

Organization

Set up a 44- × 60-yard (40 × 55 m) area. Place full-size goals at both ends. The field is divided into two zones by a midfield line. There are five field players and a keeper per team plus two neutral players. Place a supply of balls in each goal.

Procedure

1. Each team starts with three players in its defensive half and two players in its offensive half. The neutral players position themselves for a counter outlet pass. The forwards never leave their attacking half.

2. Play starts by giving possession to a team to attack as quickly as possible.

3. When the defenders or keeper win the ball, they distribute forward or wide quickly to start a counterattack.

4. One player from the defensive three can join the attack to create a numbers-up situation. The neutral players can move freely into either zone; however, only one can join in the attack at a time.

5. Let the teams play, but if there is too much buildup and slow play, then put a time restriction on scoring (must score in 6 seconds, for example).

Key Points

- The keeper must be encouraged to play quickly with her with feet or hands to create a counterattack situation.
- Discuss the risk and safety aspects of pass selection.

Goalkeeper Direct Play

Purpose

Organizing and training a teams' direct-play strategy

Organization

Set up a full field area. There are 10 players plus a goalkeeper on offense and 10 players plus a goalkeeper on defense. Place a supply of balls in each goal.

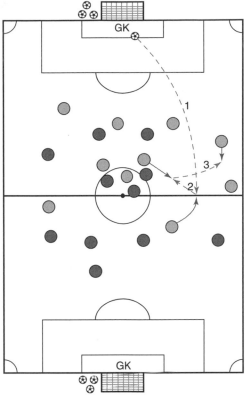

Procedure

1. Start with 11 players on the field. They pass the ball around as if they are possessing the ball out of the back. Then they play back to the keeper, who picks out one of the highest players (for example, a winger in a 1-4-3-3 system).

2. The keeper must play a fairly accurate ball, and as the ball is in flight, all of the team members must move to organize near or in the challenge area so that they will pick up the knockdown (second ball) and attack the opponent's goal. Once the players pick up the knockdown, they attack in a one- or two-touch rhythm and end up with a shot on goal.

3. Now add three defenders in the midfield. Again create possession in the back third and a long direct ball from the keeper accompanied with player movement to get around the challenge area and pick up the knockdown (there are three opponents who are also trying to get it). Continue with a one- or two-touch series for a shot on goal (and even better, a score).

4. Now add three more players in the back and do the same thing. Mix it up so that some balls come to the keeper from the six opponents so that the keeper must use punts, dropkicks, or side volleys as well as balls kicked off the ground. If the keeper has a long throw, that is also an option.

5. Now create an 11v11 environment. The 11 defenders play passive (moving, not stationary) in the beginning. As before, the attacking team starts with possession in the defensive third and then goes to a direct attack initiated by the keeper. Also, start the play with the opponent building an attack and taking a shot on goal. Now, the keeper must play from a punt, dropkick, or side volley (if the keeper possesses a very long throw, that is OK, too).

6. When satisfied, make it a live 11v11 game but with this restriction: Every time the keeper gets the ball, it is a direct service to an advanced player, with player movement to create numbers up around the ball and attacking options once the ball is picked up. These are classic direct-play tactics, but we are using them from the keeper rather than a field player. With everyone on the same page, the percentage of second-ball or knockdown wins after the initial challenge should be high, thus allowing the attacking team to generate some chances on goal. At the end, the game is all in for both teams, with an emphasis on direct play.

Key Points

- The coach should carry a ball to put in play to keep the action going. This activity needs to flow.
- All players need to stay engaged to maintain realism.

4

Attacking From the Defensive Third

Mike Noonan

"If in doubt, kick it out!" So goes the cry of stressed coaches near and far looking to get results and not concede a goal by being dispossessed close to the goal they are defending. But as the modern game is evolving, the most successful teams are measured by ball retention all over the pitch (e.g., Barcelona, Manchester United, Brazil, Akron University, and so on). This concept of ball retention is one that needs to be adopted and developed at every level of the game. It is formed on the training ground and perfected under the pressure of live matches.

Courage is a quality that coaches and managers must have and instill in their players. The most courageous action a player can take on the pitch is to want the ball and keep it. This responsibility is paramount to the success of the individual, the group (block of players around the ball), and the team. When we begin in the game, it is all about wanting the ball (U6 scrum soccer), and at the top end and as you rise in levels through the game, it is this quality that defines the level of success you will achieve. This is the essence and starting point of attacking out of the back, and it involves a mind-set that has clarity and conviction in wanting the ball.

Coaches often overlook traditional defending skills if a player possesses attacking competencies in defending roles. Balancing these skill sets is ideal, but the pendulum has swung away from defending qualifications toward attacking and possession criteria.

All attacking principles on the field must start with some consideration for the concepts of width, depth, and mobility. Which players will provide these requirements for possession to be successful? A four-back system has natural wide players in the fullbacks (many times labeled *wingbacks*), who provide width as quickly as possible to the touchline. In a three-back system, the left and right center backs can provide angled width, but this is marginalized by their defensive responsibilities to stop central attacks. They will therefore provide width in positions from the corner of the 18-yard (16 m) box to halfway to the touchline. The full width of the pitch (to touch) will usually be provided slightly upfield with wide midfielders or wingers. Depth to any attack from the defensive third is established and provided naturally by the goalkeeper and the central defenders. The forward block of players should provide length at the attacking end of the field by threatening the opponents with a direct attack behind their back line.

An alternative is a longer pass through the midfield block directly to a forward, who holds the ball while waiting for support from his teammates. Once again the decision of how to organize (system of play) the team in terms of number of players in each block will determine many of the options for attacking out of the back. With a three front or lone central striker, one would expect more holdup and link play, because the striker will normally be outnumbered by central defenders and a goalkeeper protecting and covering central space behind the defense. More often in this setup you may see some channel play to central strikers, who run behind fullbacks, who are drawn in to defend wingers, who retreat at angles to support buildup play from fullbacks and central midfielders. These would be considered direct attacks but can be effective with an active, mobile central striker to gain territory quickly and maintain possession in the opponent's half of the field.

The ultimate goal of any attacking movement in the game is to gain penetration toward the opponent's goal. Therefore, the objective of attacking out of the back must be to play through (central) or around (wide) an opponent to gain penetration. In order to achieve penetration from the back third of the field, it is the responsibility of players primarily in advance of the ball to move in order to create space for the ball to be passed or dribbled forward. Central midfield players tend to move toward the ball instinctively. However, these players must make a coordinated effort to move away from the ball to create space for their partners to move toward the ball. Wide midfield players should take up their positions in concert with the wide defenders and central midfield players. What players should avoid is creating width by lining up vertically or horizontally (square) to the ball or another player. Players who do not possess the ball should be looking for gaps behind the opponents' block of forwards and midfielders. Each time the ball is passed in possession or advanced on the dribble, the picture changes and players should move to new positions.

Another important tactical cue for players to concentrate on is their body position when receiving a ball to attack out of the back. An open body position (facing the whole field) or an advancing body position (facing forward at a minimum 45-degree angle) for defending players is crucial. These attacking body positions are visual cues for teammates to see where to play the ball. An open body also allows more choices to pass or penetrate in either direction or occasionally to turn and play backward to maintain possession.

Now that width, depth, mobility, angles of support, and body position have been assessed, the fun begins as we introduce the ball! Possibly the most important consideration in attacking out of the back is quality, range, and choice of pass in combination with the technical capability and speed to receive and prepare the ball for the next pass (or the alternative decision to penetrate by dribbling). During my career as a player and coach, one of the simplest facts of the game became evident: The highest completion rate of passing takes place when the ball is initiated from the ground. The same can be said of dribbling. Dribbling in the air (juggling) is a much more difficult technique for keeping possession or penetrating compared with dribbling on the ground.

With all these contributing factors in play, it is important to consider player attributes that are conducive to attacking out of the back. One of the most important qualities I look for in my defensive players (after their instinct to defend) is their ability to keep the ball for our team and to penetrate. Each player's ability to receive the ball under pressure and pass or run the ball out of pressure is vital to successful attacking soccer from the back. I look for central defenders who are competent with both feet but have a range of passes at their disposal to play quickly out of pressure or over distance to spring a counterattack or play through their opponent. Some of the great modern-day center backs have not been the tall bruisers of years gone by. Javier Mascherano, a converted midfielder who features for Barcelona almost exclusively as a center back, and Fabio Cannavaro, the 2006 FIFA World Player of the Year and World Cup winner, are two players both standing well under 6 feet (183 cm) tall. In my experience, the best wingbacks or fullbacks are converted forwards or wingers who have an attacking mentality. They must be able to quickly bring balls under control, run the ball at top pace, and pass the ball while moving at top pace. Additionally, there are advantages to playing the appropriate dominate-footed players on their strong side of the field. Angles and decisions are much quicker and the ability to deliver quality crosses or drive diagonal passes is predicated by this. Size again is mostly irrelevant for wingbacks, but speed is an asset that is paramount on both sides of the ball.

When considering defenders, soccer intelligence is primarily looked at in defensive terms, including how they read the opponents' attack and where danger may lie. Does the fullback tuck in appropriately to cover space behind central defenders? Do central defenders drop to delay? When do they choose to step and pressure an attacking player? However, reading the visual cues when in possession of the ball is just as important to prevent the defensive team from losing the ball and repeating their defensive roles. Can the defensive block of players recognize relevant pressure on receiving players in advance of them? Can they gauge and possess a range of passing that considers this pressure for the forward or midfield player? Can the fullback quickly and accurately analyze and exploit space to advance herself (overlap) or the ball? Does the fullback interpret angles properly so that passes can move in between blocks of the defensive opposition?

The modern game has evolved so that pure defenders are becoming rare and players with multifaceted skill sets are evolving. The final piece in this evolution from defender to attacking player must be simple mentality. Courage to want the ball is vital to any attacking theme. However, it is easier to want the ball in the attacking half of the field because the risk is less when possession is lost.

The mentality of the player from a cerebral and visceral standpoint should be a priority when coaches are selecting players to attack from the back. Training players functionally and technically is also vital to successful attacking soccer. The following exercises are designed to accomplish this. As with any exercises, use them as frameworks for a beginning and then use your coaching imagination to apply them to your environment.

Skip Pass and Ball Rotation

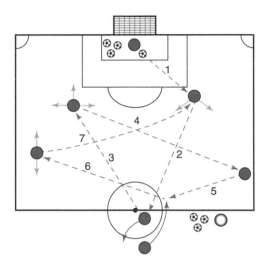

Purpose

Introducing players to playing out of the back and pattern play

Organization

Set up play on half of a standard field. There are seven players (one keeper, four defenders, and two central midfielders). Place a supply of balls in the goal. The coach is positioned just over the midfield with a supply of balls.

Procedure

1. Play starts with the goalkeeper passing the ball.
2. Players circulate the ball among themselves but may not pass to the player next to them.
3. If the ball is played to the person next to them, the two central midfield players switch so the other midfielder may receive the ball.
4. Play continues until a bad pass is made or the ball circulates out of play.
5. Play starts again from the goalkeeper.

Key Points

- Focus on quality and timing of passes and central midfielder exchange.
- Observe proper body shape in receiving the ball, facing forward whenever possible.
- The ball should circulate quickly.

GK+5v3 to 3v5+GK

Purpose

Providing players with the first steps of building play out of the back

Organization

Set up play on a standard field. Mark a centered 30-yard (27 m) zone using cones. Place a supply of balls in one goal. There are 18 total players with 5v3 plus goalkeeper in the defensive half and 3v5 plus goalkeeper in the attacking half.

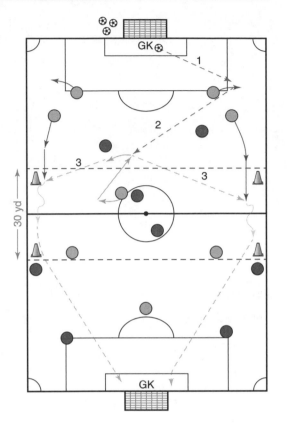

Procedure

1. Play begins with a goal-keeper in possession.

2. The keeper plus five work to maintain possession and spring a player into the middle zone. All other players do not leave their halves.

3. From the middle zone, the player serves the ball in the air to the opposite keeper, scoring 1 point for his team.

4. The other team now repeats the exercise in the opposite direction.

5. If the three players dispossess the five, they may go to goal. If they score a goal, it is worth 3 points.

Key Points

- Open up, creating a good shape to keep possession.
- Use good passing and receiving technique and body shape.
- Use crisp, sharp passing.
- Be aware of timing and quality of runs.

Variations

- The goalkeeper plus five play two touch.
- Once across the midline, one of the attacking players may go into the other half and play 4v5 to goal.

Advancing the Wingbacks to Attack

Purpose

Continuing progression and complexity of building out of the back

Organization

Set up two-thirds of a field (approximately 75 yd or 69 m) as shown, with two small goals to attack. There are four backs, two central midfielders, and a goalkeeper playing against two forwards and three midfielders.

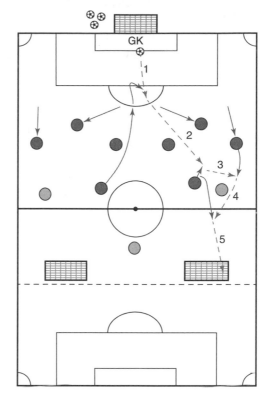

Procedure

1. Start play by playing the ball to the goalkeeper.
2. The attacking team tries to build out of the back against the defending team. The defensive midfielder must stay behind the midfield line, and only one attacker can go across midfield until the ball crosses the midfield line.
3. Attack the two small goals to score.
4. If the defending players win possession, they may go to the large goal.
5. Play continues until a goal is scored or the ball goes over either end line.

Key Points

- When the goalkeeper makes a save, the two central backs split while the two wingbacks drive up the field.
- As opposing forwards defend the central backs, the central midfielder may come back to take the ball off the goalkeeper to start an attack.
- Improvise to penetrate to small goals.

Variation

Lift territorial restrictions.

9v6 Breaking Pressure

Purpose

Exposing players to increasingly gamelike conditions while playing out of the back

Organization

Set up two-thirds of a field as shown, with a portable goal set up along the end line opposite the main goal. The attacking team positions in a 4-4-1 formation and the defending team positions in a 4-2 formation.

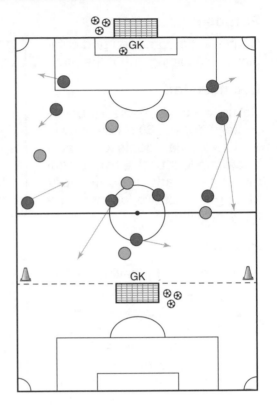

Procedure

1. The attacking team is limited to three touches.

2. The target player (one forward) must stay between midline and goal, finish one touch, or play to a teammate.

3. The attacking team cannot score until the ball crosses the midline.

4. The defending team has no restrictions and goes to goal if it intercepts play.

Key Points

- Encourage players to apply all that they have learned up until this point.
- Use good decision making coming out of the back. Find the correct player.
- Circulate the ball quickly.
- Players should have the courage to play out of the back.
- Use technical precision and good body shape.
- Take advantage of penetration opportunities while keeping possession if the penetrating play is not on.

Variations

- Add another defender (9v7).
- Take restrictions off attacking players.

Ten Attacks

Purpose

Developing a team's tactical awareness and efficiency when attacking from the defensive third

Organization

Set up play on a standard field. Use cones to create two safe zones that are the full width of the field and 35 yards (32 m) out from each end line. Organize two full teams using a formation that best suits your team (a 4-4-2 formation is shown in the diagram). Place a supply of balls in each goal.

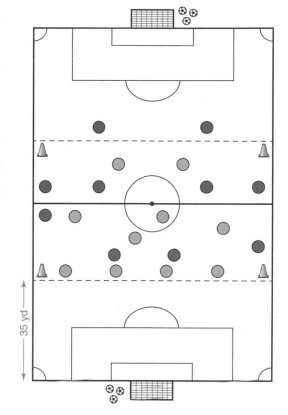

35 yd

Procedure

1. Each team gets 10 attacks against the other. Team A gets its 10 attacks first. Each attack starts from the defensive third.

2. For the first five attacks, the defending team is not allowed to enter the safe zone (35 yd [32 m] line). The attacking team may pass the ball back into the safe zone whenever it wishes to keep possession. An attack is finished when a goal is scored, a shot goes over the end line, or the defending team dispossesses the attacking team and connects five consecutive passes.

3. The second five attacks begin in the safe zone, but now three opponents may enter the zone to apply pressure.

4. One point is scored for a shot on goal and 3 points are scored for a goal.

5. After 10 attacks, the other team repeats the exercise.

Key Points

- Spread out; use the full field.
- Have patience in the attack but move the ball quickly.
- Look to create numerical advantages on the flanks and attack with speed.
- Look to control the rhythm of the game.
- Attack centrally to create space on the flanks.

Variations

- Play two attacks a man up.
- At the end of 10 attacks, each team plays an additional 20 minutes all in—no restrictions, no safe zone.

5

Attacking Through the Middle Third

Ken Lolla

Growing up in New Jersey in the 1970s provided a special soccer experience. One might wonder how an aspiring youth player in the United States at that time could experience soccer in a way that not only fueled a passion for the sport but also provided a strong base of soccer knowledge for further growth. New Jersey is a melting pot of diverse ethnic groups that carry with them a passion for the game as well as many styles of soccer. I experienced that passion and various styles of soccer, which provided an appreciation for the game on many levels.

The most influential coaches in my development were of German, English, and Scottish descent. Kerney, New Jersey, in particular had a strong Scottish community. The local club would annually host a Celtic F.C. youth team that played a number of matches during its stay. I watched and played in many Celtic youth games. The standard of play for the Celtic youth teams became the measuring stick for my growth. The work ethic, speed of play, and ability to move the ball still create vivid memories. As a youth, I never participated in a game so fast, almost always trying to catch up with the pace of the ball. Defensively, it was a challenge to ever get pressure to the Celtic players. The atmosphere of the matches was unlike anything I had felt, and it fueled my love for the sport.

Along with my experience on the field as a player, I had powerful images off the field as a spectator that equally influenced my soccer growth. I lived 45 minutes away from the Meadowlands, which was the home of the New York Cosmos of the old North American Soccer League (NASL). I grew up watching some of the world's best players, including Pelé, Franz Beckenbauer, Bogie Bogicevic, Johan Neeskens, Giorgio Chinaglia, and Carlos Alberto. Much like my experience playing against the Celtic youth team, they infused a specific style of play in my mind that forever influenced my philosophy of the game. The technical ability of the players was superior to anything I had seen. The movement of the ball was fluid and precise. There was a manipulation of the opponent through the movement of the ball and the players that provided opportunities for the Cosmos to penetrate the defense. Sitting in the stands watching this style of play game after game helped me understand the experience I had as a player against the Celtic youth team. The beauty, artistry, and cerebral aspect of their dominance was exhilarating and ignited in me a desire to perform and later coach a style that replicated those images.

What struck me most was the total team aspect of their play. Every player participated in the movement of the ball and the buildup of the attack. I had seen enough soccer to recognize the difference between a direct style of play and what I experienced watching the Cosmos. The creativity of the players, the fluidity of the game, and the buildup of the attack were not only attractive but also effective. A high priority was placed on each possession. It was clear that the team valued having the ball and every player's ability to effectively handle the ball. It was evident in this style that the midfielders, the link players, were the key.

Coincidentally, my traits as a player directed me toward the center of the game as a midfielder. Standing 5 feet, 6 inches (168 cm) and blessed with stamina and not pace, I found myself playing as a central midfielder. My limitations led me to develop my technical strengths and fostered my affinity for a style of play that includes the midfield in the buildup and execution of the attack.

Characteristics of Attacking Midfielders

When you watch the best midfielders in the world, you see certain qualities that are critical to their ability to create the attack. The most important component is their technical ability—the ability to receive and pass the ball in tight spaces under pressure. Efficient use of the ball when time is of the essence is paramount to breaking down a defense. It is one thing to be able to receive and pass; it is another to do it in the fastest time possible so as to pass time on to your teammate to create situations that provide an attacking advantage. Slow, ineffective movement of the ball in the attack gives defenders time to provide cover for each other and thus they rarely get exposed.

Second, midfielders must be aware of space on the field. Many refer to this quality as *vision*. The ability to know what is around you prior to receiving the ball provides the information needed to make appropriate decisions. Too many times, players receive a pass without knowing how much space and time they have, and they must take the time after receiving the ball to discern that information. We are constantly encouraging our players to take their eyes off the ball while it is moving from one player to another in order to evaluate the space around them. These quick looks provide the information needed to make the right decision once the player receives the ball. These quick snapshots of the field need to be trained so the eyes can view the appropriate information and the brain can determine what is important.

We train these qualities in everything we do with the ball. The passing patterns mentioned earlier provide the repetitions needed to improve technical ability as well as create vision. We also use possession and small-sided games to create an environment that forces players to move the ball so they find the space to penetrate the defense and score goals or points.

Technical Development

At the University of Louisville, we use our technical warm-up as an opportunity to train these qualities. We have implemented passing patterns as part of our warm-up and the ability to improve technique under pressure. In *The Talent Code*, author Daniel Coyle writes about the physiology of developing a skill. There are fundamental mechanisms by which the brain acquires skills. Coyle reveals that deep practice (intense, focused repetition of an exercise) promotes the development of neurons (myelin) in the brain that increase the speed and accuracy of the skill. It is only through this intense, focused repetition that the skill develops. Repetition without the concentrated intent for improvement is not effective in building the skill.

The passing patterns are set up to replicate an attacking movement. You can choose from endless shapes and movements of the passing patterns based on the movements you are attempting to encourage for your team. The pattern requires a passing action and then movement into another position within the pattern. There are usually two to three players along with multiple balls at each position in case the pattern breaks down due to an errant pass or touch.

The key to developing the skills of passing and receiving is to increase the speed of the pattern beyond where the players are comfortable. It is not effective to simply get the ball around the pattern without making a mistake. The key is to constantly encourage the players to do it faster. Inevitably this will force some mistakes as the players move and think beyond their comfort zone, but it is in this environment where the deep practice takes place. We also often use three or four balls in a pattern. The constant repetition does not allow for a mental break and forces the attention of the player on the exercise and the skills necessary to be successful.

The words we use in reminding the players of the habits they need are critical to their development. First, we use words to reinforce the movements we want to develop. The habit of looking around prior to receiving the ball is difficult for young players, but it is critical for midfielders, where space and time is limited. We are constantly asking the players to *look* for the next player involved in the pattern before receiving a pass. The best midfielders in the world, such as Xabi Alonso and Andres Iniesta, are always turning their head to find space, their teammates, and their opponents. This ability to receive information with a simple look and decide where to move and what ball to play next is one we can develop.

We also encourage the players to *move* for each pass, constantly creating the best angles for the player passing the ball. The movement into space is important in a game that is so fluid. Young players especially get caught watching only the ball and find themselves as spectators until the ball arrives at their feet, and then they are forced into making a decision that they are not prepared to make. Having a *look* and *moving* into space help prepare them for the next play.

Two phrases we often use to encourage an increase in the speed of the activity are *play the correct foot* and *pass time on*. Many times players are content to simply get the ball to the next player. Which foot they play to will help the receiving player with the efficiency of the next pass. If the ball is played to the lead foot, it will help the player deliver the next pass sooner and increase the speed of play. When the ball is played behind a player, it takes more touches and time to deliver the next pass. Likewise, the speed at which the player plays the pass will determine how much time the receiving player has to make the next decision. If the ball is played lazily at a slow pace, the next player will have less time due to closing defenders. A sharp pass with pace, when *played to the correct foot*, provides the receiving player with more time to make the next play, thus *passing time on*. Encouraging the players to make firmer passes also develops the receiving ability of their teammates.

Finally, forcing the speed of the exercise beyond the players' comfort zone inevitably results in mistakes. Encouragement to get on with the *next play* is an important mental skill. If a pass is off target or a touch is heavy, the players are encouraged to solve the problem and get the ball to the next player as soon as possible. The extra balls around the grid allow the players to get the next ball going if one is lost. Too often the players stay focused on the mistake and miss the opportunity to move to the next play. The players who move to the next play the quickest are always the most effective in the exercise and the game. The speed of the exercise does not allow time for negative self-talk; the next play is coming too quickly to lament a bad pass or poor touch.

We have found the passing patterns to be effective in developing the attacking skills necessary for all our players, especially our midfielders. In a 15-minute period, we run the exercise for 1 to 3 minutes at a time, with a break of 1 to 2 minutes with stretching movements in between to allow for physical recovery as well as continue the warm-up process. In this length of time, each player gets 50 to 80 contacts with the ball. Each contact is an opportunity for them to develop the qualities necessary to deal with the ball under pressure.

Tactical Development

Presently, there is no team better than Barcelona in the effective and efficient use of the ball. Due to Barcelona's incredible ability to maintain possession, they force most teams to defend with large numbers closer to their own goal. It is Barcelona's use of time and space in the movement of the ball that allows them to keep possession and effectively penetrate the defense for quality attempts on goal.

The passing patterns are a great tool for developing the individual qualities of each player to deal with the demands of playing in the midfield. Group and team games are essential for developing the tactics necessary for breaking down a defense, resulting in opportunities on goal. Tactics are determined by so many factors that constantly change the demands of the game. Certainly, your team's philosophy will dictate the style and tactical demands heading into the game. Likewise, the opponent, the score, and the time left in the game will influence what is required of your team.

Training midfielders to be effective puts an emphasis on technical ability and dealing with less time and space. The game has progressed to include more players in the midfield. Tactically, putting more players in the midfield forces the attacking team to either be more direct in bypassing the large numbers or be creative and effective enough in moving the ball to break down the mass of midfield players. This ability to break down the opponent often requires the technical ability to play in tight spaces.

We will discuss two basic styles of play that cover most tactical scenarios for midfielders. First and most commonly seen in the modern game is when teams defend closer to their own goal and use the space behind the opponent to attack the goal. Attacking from a position closer to your own goal requires the ability to move at speed to counterattack the opposition. When you defend closer to your own goal, you decrease the space to play for the opponents, making it more difficult to create scoring opportunities. Likewise, defending closer to your own goal creates more space to attack once you win the ball. The key is using the space while it is available and the opponent is still exposed.

The second style of play is the tactics of extended possession. This style is used to break down the defense of a team that gets everyone back behind the ball quickly to prevent counterattacks. Fast, efficient movement of the ball is essential to open gaps in an organized defense. Quickly changing the point of attack creates opportunities to play penetrating passes to target players or to make penetrating runs.

Training the team, and in particular midfielders, to play forward quickly is critical for the success of counterattacking soccer. With the opponent in a forward attacking position, the first ball forward has the potential to eliminate many of the opponents in defending the counterattack. Most teams employing counterattacking tactics play with one forward. Once in possession, finding the forward (or any player in an advanced position) with the earliest ball is often the most effective pass in starting the counterattack.

An exercise we use in training the players to play forward early is a possession game that is directional with target players at each end. The grid is rectangular, with the direction of the game played lengthwise, and the size depends on the number, age, and skill level of the players involved. Manipulation of the size dictates the effects of the training; a narrower field forces the play to be more direct, whereas widening the field allows for more space to play indirectly. To replicate game situations as much as possible, I recommend teams of at least four. With younger players especially, it is important to play with neutral players to help in maintaining possession and provide maximum opportunities for growth.

Possession to Targets

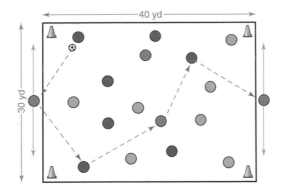

Purpose

Developing effective techniques and tactics of possession in order to penetrate

Organization

Set up a 30- × 40-yard (27 × 37 m) area. There are seven players on each team plus two neutral players. The numerical advantage with neutral players provides the extra options in attack to ensure more success. On each end line is a target player, who plays with the team in possession. This player may move laterally along the end line to create the best position to receive a pass. Place a supply of balls on one sideline near the coach.

Procedure

1. Play starts with one team in possession. It restarts with a quick kick-in by the team earning possession when the opponents touch the ball out of bounds.
2. The team in possession scores a point by playing into the target area at both ends of the grid in succession while maintaining possession.
3. Play continues even after a point is scored. It is possible for one team to score several points in a row.
4. Play is usually limited to two touch. Target and neutral players may be limited to one touch. The coach makes the proper adjustment for the skill level of the players.

Key Points

- The emphasis of the exercise is for the team in possession to recognize when it is appropriate to play the target, execute the play, and support the target once the ball is played forward. The ability to deliver a quality pass under pressure will determine the possibility of starting a successful counterattack.

- Moving forward at good angles of support to receive the ball off the forward is critical to continuing the attack forward.

- This activity promotes continuous transition and the importance of mentally making the transition from defending to attacking. In the modern game with only one forward, numbers must be added out of midfield to create opportunities and unbalance the defense.

- The timing and speed of the movement forward is critical; it is often in transition that the game is decided.

Find the Forward and Go

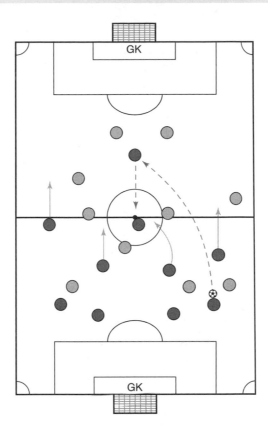

Purpose

Encouraging counterattacking habits in midfielders

Organization

Set up a full-size field for an 11v11 tactical team session. Although this game does not need to be 11v11, the numbers should allow the teams to play in three lines to promote functional play among the forward, midfield, and defense. Adjust the field size if you are training fewer players.

Procedure

1. An attacking team (A) starts in possession of the ball. The other team (B) defends in a counterattacking position, closer to its own goal.

2. When the defending team dispossesses the attacking team, it gets a free opportunity to play the first pass into the forward without being obstructed. The forward must receive it in an onside position and has only two touches to connect with the midfielders in support.

3. Once the ball is connected to the forward, the original attacking team begins to defend the counter.

Key Points

- This exercise resembles game situations and makes the training more functional according to positions.

- This exercise encourages the midfielders to look forward first once they win possession. Likewise, with the forward allowed only two touches, the midfielders must move in support to maintain possession and continue the counter.

- Once the defending team gets behind the ball and limits the space to play, it is important for the attacking team to break down the opponent by moving the ball quickly. To maintain possession in the opponent's half, where time and space are at a premium, requires efficient movement of the ball. Finding and creating the space to penetrate takes patience and is often less direct. Training the midfielders to effectively use space is critical in being successful in the attacking half.

Variations

- The progression of the exercise is to allow team A to defend the passer once the ball is lost in possession, still allowing the forward to receive the ball once it is delivered. This step forces the midfielders to combine to create the first passing opportunity to the forward. If the first player to win possession is closed down and does not have the opportunity to play forward, supporting players must stay involved in the play and create the next possible opportunity. Again, the emphasis should be placed on how quickly they can play forward.

- Finally, the game can continue live, so once team B loses the ball, it is forced to get back behind the ball into a counterattacking position. In this case, when the game is live, only when the ball is won in its own half is team B given a free ball into the forward.

Multiple-Goal Game

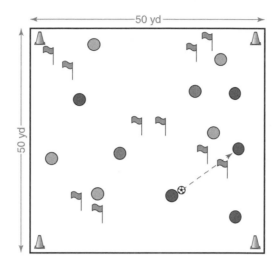

Purpose

Training efficient ball movements and possession

Organization

Set up a 50- × 50-yard (46 × 46 m) playing area with five flag goals equally spaced throughout the area. For younger players, it may be more effective to use more goals than the number of players on each team in order to create more options for the attacking team. There are two teams of five players and two neutral players.

Procedure

1. Play starts by the coach tossing a ball into the playing area for either team to gain possession.
2. Points are scored by passing the ball through any of the flag goals to another teammate. Neutral players may pass and receive balls through the goals as well.
3. Play continues even when a point is scored. Consecutive points cannot be scored in the same goal.

Key Points

- This game encourages the attacking teams to move the ball and find the goal that is the most open for scoring the point.
- Recognition of when the opponent has compacted one area of the field and limited space to penetrate will encourage the attacking team to change the point of attack, finding more space and better opportunities to penetrate the defense. This must happen quickly through visual recognition as well as technical movement off the ball. This exercise is excellent for training those qualities.

Six-Goal Game

Purpose

Training functional possession

Organization

Set up a playing area that is 60 yards (55 m) wide and 50 yards (46 m) long with three flag goals equally spaced along each end line. One goal is central and the other two are evenly spaced on each side to force the defensive team to defend a wider area of the field. There are two teams of 10 players each.

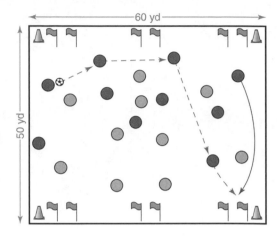

Procedure

1. Play is directional, with each team defending three goals.

2. The attacking team can score on any of the opponent's three goals, providing the opportunity to move the ball and unbalance the defense to create the best opportunity to attack a goal.

3. With each team defending set goals, the players are now in positions related to the game. The functional aspect of this game is valuable because players have the opportunity to make decisions in relation to their positions on the field.

Key Points

• This environment is valuable as midfield play in the modern game, but it is not limited to midfielders. So many times outside backs join the midfield to create width and unbalance the defense. Likewise, forwards are found dropping into midfield to find the ball and lose defenders.

• Allow for the movement of players in relation to their positions while creating numerous attacking opportunities and decisions.

• It is critical that players, particularly midfielders, develop the ability to adjust to the demands of the game. The opponent, score, and time left in the match often dictate what is needed, both defensively and in the attack.

• Technical ability, efficiency with the ball, field awareness, and vision are essential to playing in the midfield. These exercises help develop these qualities to make midfielders more effective in the attack.

Score in Five to Survive

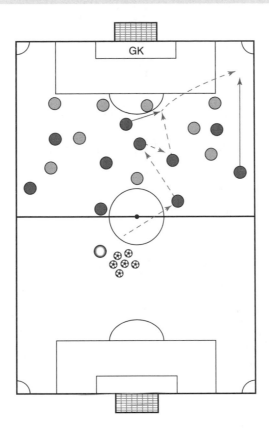

Purpose

Training functional possession against a withdrawn defense

Organization

Set up a training area using half of a regulation-size field. The team defending the goal has 9 field players plus a keeper. The attacking team has 10 field players. The defensive team defends in a GK-4-4-1 formation. The attacking team attacks in a 4-5-1 formation. The coach is positioned centrally just outside the training area with a supply of balls.

Procedure

1. Play starts by the coach passing a ball to the offensive team.
2. The attacking team has 5 minutes to score. If the team does not score in that time, the defense wins.
3. A new ball is played to the offense quickly when the ball leaves the training area or the keeper gains possession.

Key Points

- Move the ball quickly from side to side to open gaps in the defense.
- Quick combination play in the center will draw the defense to the middle, creating space wide.
- Use overlapping players on the flanks to get behind the defense to serve a dangerous ball into the center.
- If the defensive players win the ball, press them immediately to regain possession.
- As soon as a new ball is put into play, get it moving.
- Play with a sense of controlled urgency.

Variations

- Use team formations best suited to prepare for your next game.
- Lengthen the time to score a goal.
- Use a scoring points system such as 3 points for a goal, 1 point for a shot on goal for offense, or 1 point for keeping possession for six passes in a row for defense.
- Depending on the age and level of play, you may use fewer defensive players.

6

Creating Opportunities in the Attacking Third

John Hackworth

In our last game of group play during the 2009 Confederations Cup in South Africa, the U.S. Men's National Team needed to beat Egypt by four or more goals (and get some help from Brazil against Italy) in order to advance to the semifinals. Scoring four goals is difficult at any level, but in a FIFA competition it is extremely challenging. Needless to say, we knew that we needed to somehow create numerous chances if we were going to score four or more goals.

Egypt was a very good defensive team. In their system, they often deployed five defenders. In the tournament so far, Egypt had only allowed two goals. They narrowly lost to Brazil (1–0) on a late penalty kick and surprisingly upset Italy (2–1) by coming from behind. We knew that it was going to be an extremely tough game, but we were committed to attacking from the start. To paraphrase a line from the movie *Dumb and Dumber*, "So you're saying we have a chance" became our battle cry in the days leading up to the game. Long story short, we beat Egypt 4–0 and advanced, beating Spain in the semifinals and eventually losing to Brazil in the final. This is an extraordinary example, but the point is that our team knew going into the game that we needed to create opportunities in a variety of ways. We prepared with that mentality and were ultimately successful.

Throughout my coaching career, I have been extremely fortunate to have had incredible mentors (Walt Chyzowych, Bob Gansler, Jay Miller, Jay Vidovich, John Ellinger, Bruce Arena, Bob Bradley, and Peter Nowak, to name just a few) who shared with me their philosophies on the beautiful game. Each of these mentors had his own ideas and philosophies of the game and how it should be played. While learning and studying under these coaches, I stole sessions, activities, and management ideas that I knew I could use with my own teams. Along the way, I used much of what I was taught as I developed my own philosophies as a coach.

These fundamental principles and beliefs have allowed me to be successful at many levels. I have coached youth, college, professional, and national teams. I have been in charge of World Cup qualifiers where we had to win in extremely hostile environments. I have had teams that made dramatic comebacks in the final moments of games. Fortunately or not, I have somehow been involved in far too many important games where my team needed to score multiple goals. At the same time, I have always believed that the performance of my team is as important as the result. In particular, when I have coached children, I have always put the emphasis on player development over team results.

The combination of these two conflicting ideas has always challenged me as a coach. Should I coach my teams to win? Or should I prepare them to perform with a certain style? Ultimately, I believe that you can do both, because if your teams are well prepared and schooled in the attacking fundamentals of the game, then the results will follow. Therefore, regardless of the team or age group, my fundamental philosophy has always been to create a training environment where my players learn the skills that allow them to unlock the key ideas to attacking soccer.

As I am sure you have discovered yourself, you can't score unless you are able to create numerous opportunities in the attacking third. Although that is the focus of this chapter, creating an effective attacking team that can execute in the final third is not something that is accomplished easily. In fact, it is probably the most difficult concept to teach your team. The main reason is that in order to create opportunities in the attacking third, your team needs to be proficient in all the demands of the game. The good news is that you can train your team to be creative and effective in the final third, and in doing so, your team will improve in the middle and defensive thirds of the field as well. The challenge is in creating a training program that consistently (daily) teaches your players the skill sets, ideas, physical tools, and mental approach necessary for executing this type of attack.

In this chapter, we focus on teaching players to attack in a variety of ways. They need to be able to execute combination play, including one-two passes (wall passes), overlapping runs, and double passes. They need to practice creating numerical advantages in certain areas by getting players forward into the attack. They need to be able to execute penetrating dribbling runs, long-range shots, and quality service into the box. At the same time, the players' movement off the ball is equally important. They need to be able to recognize when to make smart penetrating runs behind the defensive line and when to hold and even check back for the ball. When the ball is about to be served from wide areas, the timing of near- and far-post runs in the box is critical. That's pretty much it. Easy, right? Well, it is always much easier said than done, and there is even more to it. We could go on and on, but we will focus on these key ideas in the following sections of in this chapter.

Looking back at that 2009 Confederations Cup game against Egypt, we were fortunate to score four goals against such a quality opponent. No matter what the situation is or how well you have prepared your team, scoring four goals in a game is tough. However, it is my belief that if you consistently coach your players to have an attacking mentality in training and teach them the skill sets and ideas to do so, you will produce a team that at the minimum will create numerous opportunities in the final third. In the end, that attacking style will serve them well in all competitions.

One-Twos

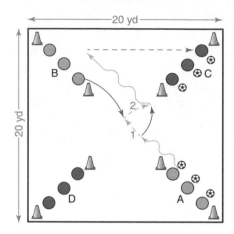

Purpose

Developing proper technical and tactical execution of one-two passes (wall passes)

Organization

Set up a 20- × 20-yard (18 × 18 m) playing area. Two teams of six players are organized behind four cones as shown.

Procedure

1. The first player in line A at bottom right starts the move by running with the ball toward the middle of the grid and plays into the first player in line B at top left, who has checked to the middle of the grid.
2. The line A player then makes a quick move toward line C, off the ball, to get the ball back.
3. The line A player then changes direction with his first touch to dribble through to the back of line B and then rolls the ball to team C at top right.
4. As soon as the player from line A has cleared out, the first player in line C at top right starts the same move and eventually combines with line D at bottom left.
5. Play continues, alternating in both directions.
6. Once the players have the rhythm of the movements down, they can go to goal on both ends of the grid.

Key Points

- The player dribbles with close control and creates space.
- Be aware of the timing and angle of the supporting player (i.e., wall player).
- Be aware of the pace and accuracy of the pass into the wall player while accelerating into the space behind the defender.
- Perfect the execution of the one-touch pass from the wall player into the path of the receiving player.
- Use visual communication.

Variations

- Add defenders.
- Place goals 12 to 18 yards (11-16 m) from the end lines with a goalkeeper in each goal. After the one-two exchange, the player in possession may shoot on goal.
- Play a game of 6v6 plus keepers on an appropriately sized field. A goal is worth 1 point and a goal scored off a one-two pass is worth 3 points.

Overlap

Purpose

Developing proper technical and tactical execution of an overlap

Organization

Set up a 20- × 20-yard (18 × 18 m) playing area. Two teams of six players are organized behind four cones as shown.

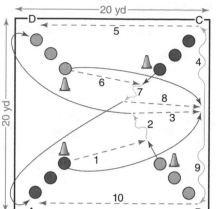

Procedure

1. The first player in line A at bottom left starts the move with a square pass to the first player in line B at bottom right.

2. The line B player then takes a few quick touches toward the middle of the grid, leaving space for the player who played her the ball to overlap her.

3. The line B player then plays the ball into the path of the line A player, who dribbles to the back of line C. She then rolls the ball across to the back of line D.

4. Play then restarts from the top of the diagram in the opposite direction. The first player in line D at the top of the diagram can initiate play as soon as the line A player from the bottom has received the ball. The player from line D plays the ball to the player from line C, who dribbles toward the center as the line D player overlaps. The line C player plays to the line D player, who dribbles to the back of line B and then plays the ball to the back of line A.

Key Points

- Initiate overlap with movement off the touch (pass).
- Use accuracy and proper weight on the initial pass.
- Use a receiving touch that creates space for the overlapping player.
- Be aware of the timing and execution of the layoff pass.
- Use visual communication.

Variations

- Add defenders.
- Place goals 12 to 18 yards (11-16 m) from the end lines. After an overlap, the player in possession may shoot on goal.
- Play a game of 6v6 plus keepers on an appropriately sized field. A goal is worth 1 point and a goal scored after an overlap is worth 3 points.

Double Pass

Purpose

Developing proper technical and tactical execution of a double pass

Organization

Set up a playing area in front of goal as shown. There are two lines of three players positioned 10 yards (9 m) from the penalty area. Each line has a supply of balls. Two additional players position 8 yards (7 m) away from and facing the line of players. There is a shadow defender who positions behind these two additional players. A goalkeeper is in the goal.

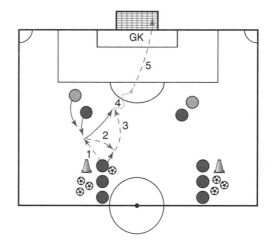

Procedure

1. Play starts when the first player in line executes a double pass with the forward who is marked by the shadow defender.
2. Once the play is made, the player who acted as the shadow defender becomes the attacker who is checking back for the ball.
3. The attacker, who just checked back for the ball and had a shot on goal, goes to the end of the passing line.
4. The player who first made the entry pass then becomes the shadow defender after his turn.
5. The two lines should alternate in quick succession. As soon as the first player shoots, the other line initiates play.

Key Points

- Initiate the pass by showing (checking) for the ball.
- Be aware of the rhythm and timing of the passes (weight and pace).
- Immediate movement of the receiving player off his touch into the space behind.
- Be aware of the timing and playing of the third (through ball) pass.

Variations

- Add defenders.
- Play 6v6 plus keepers on an appropriately sized field. A goal is worth 1 point and a goal scored after a double pass is worth 3 points.
- Add one or two neutral players.

Four-Goal Shooting on the Run

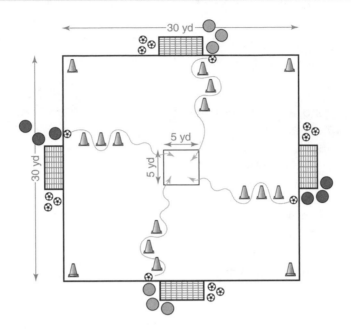

Purpose

Developing proper technical execution of dribble penetration and then a shot from distance

Organization

Set up a 30- × 30-yard (27 × 27 m) area with a mini goal or target on each sideline and a 5- × 5-yard (5 × 5 m) square centered inside the area. Place three cones with approximately 1 yard (1 m) between each at the left of each goal. There is a group of three players at each of the four goals, and each group has a supply of balls.

Procedure

1. Players start to the side of their goal.
2. On the coach's command, the first player in each line dribbles a ball with fast feet through cones out to the center square, avoids the other players, and shoots into the opposite goal.
3. After shooting, the players return to their goal. As they arrive, the next player in line can race out.
4. Play is repeated.
5. Make sure players stand on both sides of their goal to retrieve missed shots.

Key Points

- Dribble and shoot as quickly as possible.
- Be aware of body shape, off-center approaches to the ball, contact on the ball, and follow-through.
- Use proper finishing technique.
- Shoot quickly.

Variations

- Make the drill into a competitive game where teams have 90 seconds to score as many goals as possible.
- Players shoot on their own goal. Before shooting, the attacker must dribble to the center square, return back toward his goal, and exchange a pass with a teammate who is next in line or positioned wide.

Three-Man Combinations to Goal

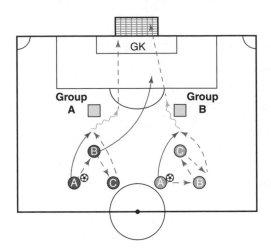

Purpose

Developing technical execution of three-man combinations resulting in a penetration dribble and a shot from distance

Organization

Set up half of a standard field. Two groups of three players set up in a triangle, with the forward 5 yards (5 m) in front of a defensive mannequin that is placed 5 yards (5 m) outside the penalty for each group. The players forming the triangle are 8 to 10 yards (7-9 m) apart. Place a supply of balls near each group.

Procedure

Group A and group B alternate attempts on goal and execute various combinations to attack the space in front of, beside, or behind the defensive mannequins, as follows.

Group A

1. Player A passes to player B and runs behind player B toward goal.
2. Player B passes to player C, who finds player A with a through ball.
3. Player A dribbles hard inside the dummy and shoots on goal.
4. Players B or C must follow up in the box for any rebounds.

Group B

1. Player A passes to player B and overlaps.
2. Player B passes to player C.
3. Player C passes back to player B, who finds player A with a through ball.
4. Player A dribbles hard at the dummy and shoots at goal.
5. Player C follows up in the box for any rebounds.

Key Points

- The quality of passes must be good (especially the weight of the pass).
- Emphasize the quality of touch on the dribble and the final preparation before the shot.
- Use good shooting technique.
- The goalkeeper reads the play, trying to prevent a goal.
- Train at the speed of a live game.
- Concentrate on the quality of the shot and a possible follow-up rebound.

Variations

- Players may change roles within the triangle.
- Replace the defensive mannequin with a live defender. Make the drill competitive. The team that scores the most goals in a set time wins.

Three-Goal Numerical Advantage Game

Purpose

Understanding how to create numerical advantages

Organization

Set up an area on a standard field as shown in the diagram. The size can be adjusted depending on age and skill level. There are two teams of eight players each plus four players for each team on the touchlines (two in the attacking half and two in the defending half each). Set up three flag goals along each end line.

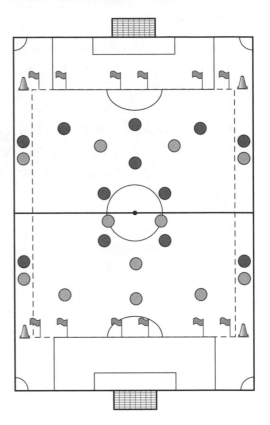

Procedure

1. One team attacks three goals and the other team defends three goals.

2. If the ball is played to a wide player on the touchline, that player can join in and create a numbers-up advantage. As soon as the team loses possession, the extra player must leave the field.

3. A goal is scored if a player dribbles through a goal cleanly.

Key Points

- Look to bring in players to go numbers up.
- Recognize when to keep possession versus when to attack a goal.
- Be aware that the quicker the ball moves side to side, the quicker spaces will open up to attack.

Variations

- Play unlimited touch, two touch, or one touch (except wide players, who play two touch).
- Require players to go side to side before they can attack.

Overlapping to Score

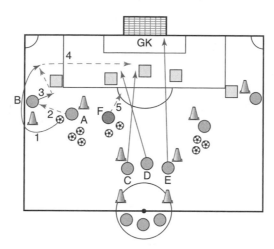

Purpose

Creating a numerical advantage with an overlap combined with crossing and finishing

Organization

Set up play in half of a standard field. Place five mannequins in the defensive quarter of the field. First, place one mannequin on each flank, 25 yards (23 m) from the end line and 10 yards (9 m) off the touchline. Then place the remaining three mannequins in the goal area—two should be 15 yards (14 m) directly out and in line with each goalpost and the third should be on the penalty spot. Two offensive players are on each flank with a supply of balls. Three offensive central players are positioned 35 yards (32 m) from goal. An additional three forwards are waiting at midfield to rotate into the drill. The coach is positioned centrally 35 yards (32 m) from goal with a supply of balls.

Procedure

1. Player A passes to player B, who takes an aggressive touch inside past a dummy.
2. Player A overlaps player B, and player B plays a return pass to the corner for player A to cross.
3. Players C, D, and E vary their runs (near post, central, and far post) with speed and timing to finish.
4. After an attempt on goal, the coach then plays a ball to the top of the box to the first of the three attackers to react to her. That forward executes a quick turn and finish.
5. Incorporate a recovery run for player A back to his line to repeat the same action on the same flank or alternate left and right flanks.

Key Points

- Make an aggressive first touch past the dummy.
- Use change of speed of the overlapping player and weight of the pass to the crosser.
- Be aware of the timing of the near- and far-post runs.
- Be aware of the angle of the runs.
- React to receive the ball from the coach.

Variations

- Alternate attacks from the left and right flanks.
- Vary the pass combination on the flank to create a penetrating run for a cross.
- Make the drill competitive by requiring 10 attacks each for the left- and right-flank players; the most goals scored wins.
- Replace 3 central mannequin defenders with 2 live defenders.

3v2 to 4v3 Transition

Purpose

Understanding how to create numerical advantages in the final third

Organization

Set up a 50- × 40-yard (46 × 37 m.) playing area with a clear midfield line and goals at each end. The attacking team has two lines of players 10 yards (9 m) apart on one side of their goal. A third line is on the other side of the goal near the touchline. There are three or four players in each of the three lines. The defending team has two lines of players on their end line, 5 yards (5 m) wide of each goalpost. There are three or four players in each line and there are two neutral players on the touchlines at midfield. Each team has a goalkeeper.

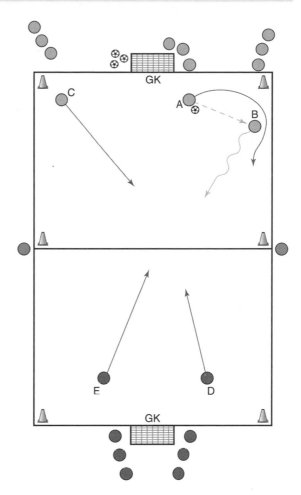

Procedure

1. Play starts with player A playing to player B and overlapping her while player C joins in the attack.
2. On first touch, players D and E sprint off the posts to defend.
3. Players A, B, and C attack the goal of players D and E. If D and E win the ball, or the keeper makes a save, they immediately outlet pass to a neutral player, who joins the attack 4v3 versus players A, B, and C. Neutral players can only attack.
4. The ball is in play until it leaves the field or a goal is scored.
5. Play restarts with the next three attackers 3v2 as before. Rotate players F and G every 2 minutes.

Key Points

- Use the numbers advantage quickly.
- Attack the space with speed; commit the defender.
- Make a quick transition from offense to defense and vice versa.
- Use good decision making on the final pass or shot.

Variations

- Play the game for 8 minutes. Teams switch and play another 8-minute game. The most goals scored overall wins.
- Adjust the length of the games to suit the number of players and the size of the field.

Pattern Play to Goal

Purpose

Creating functional technical and tactical pattern play in the final third

Organization

Set up play on half of a standard field. This activity requires functional organization of the front six attacking players (shown in a 4-3-3 system). There is also one goalkeeper. The coach is at midfield with a supply of balls.

Procedure

Place the players in the positions you would like them in throughout the final third of the field. The coach passes the ball to a midfielder, who starts a fundamental pattern that consists of a six-pass sequence. The sequence includes penetrating passes, dribble penetration, runs off the ball, timing of runs in the box, the final pass, and a finish on goal, as follows:

1. The first pass is from the deepest midfielder to a more attacking midfielder.
2. The second pass is returned to the original midfielder, who has moved into a good supporting (angled) position.
3. The third pass is a through ball to the third midfielder, who has advanced forward. This midfielder takes several touches toward goal (committing the defenders).
4. The third midfielder then slots a through ball to the wide attacking player, who has timed his run and will receive the ball behind the defenders. This player takes the necessary touches toward the end line (last touch is a preparation touch).
5. The player then provides the final pass back and across the goalmouth to attacking players making runs in the box.
6. The striker finishes on goal.

After the attacking players understand the pattern, progress the activity by adding both defensive and attacking players. I like to do this activity with two separate attacking groups. Normally, I progress the patterns through the various options and eventually let the players improvise the patterns they execute. If you have enough players, you can build this session up using the two attacking groups and then combining them on a full field. Finally, end the session with an 11v11 game.

Key Points

- Alternate the direction that the pattern follows to goal.
- Use high-quality passes.
- Make sure passes are played to the proper foot (the foot that will be away from the defender).
- Be aware of the timing of runs. Passes and running should be at game pace.

Variations

- Execute a wall pass with a target forward.
- Lay off from the target forward with a shot from distance.
- Require inside dribble penetration and then a diagonal through ball.
- Add overlapping runs from the outside back.
- Add more attacking and defending players.
- Encourage patterns that play to the strengths of your individual players.

7

Attacking From the Flanks

Dean Wurzberger

Attacking from the wide areas remains an important aspect of successful team play. With many teams now choosing to defend with a majority of their players recovering into deep positions in their own half, attacking from the flanks is an important tactic to pull defenders out from the central areas in order to create attacking spaces in front of the goal.

For many years, the role of wingers was to provide width for their team when in possession so they could receive the ball and deliver crosses to central attackers in the penalty area. Attacking from the flanks has evolved over time, and the days of wingers who started in wide positions and mostly stayed in those wing positions throughout the game are largely over.

One of the trends among today's top teams is to have wide attackers who take up starting positions in a wide area and then play from the wing. Rather than remaining in fixed wide positions, wide attackers today make numerous well-timed runs from the wing into central areas, which can cause a number of problems for the opponent's defense. This tactic makes defending wide attackers all the more difficult when they possess good mobility and run laterally as well as vertically.

Wide attackers who move inside often draw the opponent's wide defenders as the defenders mark them and move inside with them, thus creating space in the wing area. Fullbacks and central midfield players for the team in possession often overlap into these open wing spaces and then assume the role of the winger. They are often relied upon to cross the ball accurately into the penalty area.

Crossing the ball always has been and always will be an important part of effective wing play. Delivering the ball accurately into the penalty area requires a great deal of skill and needs to be practiced on a regular basis. Most players should be able to cross the ball on a run.

A good cross either hits a key space in the penalty area or picks out a teammate in a good attacking position while eliminating the goalkeeper. There are three main target areas for crosses, all of which should be delivered to the area near the edge of the goal:

1. The *near-post cross*, which is for a first-time header, direct shot on goal, or redirect to the back-post area
2. The *far-post cross*, which often results in a header or volley back across the goalkeeper to the far-post area or a header near post
3. The *mid-goal-area cross*, where attacking players could get free into that dangerous central position

Another effective option to deliver a crossing ball from the wing, especially when the wide attacker has arrived in a deep position near the opponent's goal line, is to cut the ball back along the ground for oncoming attackers making forward runs. This cutback pass is especially dangerous because attacking players cannot be offside since the ball is ahead of them and then played backward. Another advantage of this type of low cross delivery is that attackers meeting such a pass often only need a one-touch contact on the ball to produce a quality scoring chance.

The two key areas for delivering crosses into the penalty area are as follows:

1. Area just wide of the penalty-box sideline and 6 to 18 yards (5-16 m) from the goal (early cross)
2. Area within 6 yards (5 m) of the goal line (deep or byline cross)

The most effective types of crosses are as follows:

- Crosses played early into the spaces behind the opponent's defense
- Crosses that bend away from the goalkeeper and into the path of players making runs
- Crosses hit with the proper weight or pace that allow runners to judge the cross and thus adjust the timing of their runs accordingly

The most effective scoring techniques from crosses are headers, volleys, and normal shots off the ground once a crossed ball drops back down to ground level. How a team gets into crossing positions and creates opportunities to attack from the wing is another important consideration. There are three main game situations for creating these wing attacking opportunities: flow of the game, development of overloads, and combination play.

Flow of the Game

- *Central to wide-area movement of the ball:* During good attacking play when a team in possession of the ball builds play out from its defensive third, players normally spread out and provide width and depth in attack. This type of offensive shape creates opportunities to play the ball to players taking up wide positions. In addition, most defending teams will recover to protect central positions as a priority, which often leaves attacking players in wide positions without tight marking.

Good possession play among attacking players in the central areas of the field also draws the opponent's defense toward the middle.

- *Switching play:* Another effective team tactic to get the ball into wide positions is to switch the play. Switching the play means attacking down one side of the field and then quickly and efficiently switching the play to other side of the field.

- *Counterattack:* Counterattacks have always been tactically significant in the scoring of goals. The top teams today score more than 40 percent of their goals as a direct result of counterattacking play. Players attacking from the flanks during a counterattack often receive the ball in the space deep down the wing and then look for support players in central areas to feed with crossing passes on the ground. In addition, depending upon the speed of the defensive recovery, it may be possible for an attacker collecting the ball in a wide area on the counterattack to dribble the ball at speed straight to the goal for a shot.

- *Regains:* Regaining possession of the ball through a challenge, tackle, or interception can take place in wide areas of the field and consequently lead to wing attacking opportunities. Many team defending strategies feature a compact central block of players positioned in the middle of the field in order to deflect attacks into wide areas. When the ball is forced into wide areas by an organized defense, challenging for possession and pressing the ball in wide areas often result. Regaining possession on the wing provides immediate counterattack opportunities, which could lead to creating quality chances to score goals.

Development of Overloads

- *Overlaps:* Overlapping runs made by players behind the ball that exploit spaces created by wide attackers moving inside with and without the ball have been an effective attacking movement for many years. If done properly, the overlapping player can create a 2v1 overload situation against an opponent's fullback. Most overlaps are made by fullback or central midfield players.

- *Underlaps:* The underlap is an attacking movement similar to the overlap, but the run forward is made inside the wide attacker in possession. Set up much like an overlap, the back-line defender would play the ball to a wide attacker and tell her to hold it up while she makes a run down the wing inside the teammate in possession and behind the marking defender.

- *Inside-to-out diagonal runs:* Running diagonally from central areas into wide spaces is another effective way to create an overload on the wing. In most cases, these runs are made by forwards or midfield players who are looking to attack spaces that will be difficult for the opponent to cover. Many times central players will make diagonal runs to the wing when their team has possession in their defending half of the field, giving back-line players in possession an option to play a longer pass into spaces behind the defense.

- *Forwards pulling wide:* Another way to create an overload in the wing area is to have a forward pulling out into wing positions. Forwards often use this type of run to exploit the space between members of the opponent's back line. Forwards will look for space between their marking center back and the near fullback on the ball side.

Combination Play

- *Movements to receive the ball:* Wide players must become skilled at creating space for themselves with quick and intelligent movement off the ball. These movements are often called *checking runs* and are needed to get the wide players free from marking players in order to receive a pass. Two examples of how a wide attacker can get free from tight marking are (1) checking back deep toward the ball and then spinning off and sprinting into the space behind the marking fullback, looking for a pass down the wing behind the defending full-back, and (2) moving away from the ball initially when a teammate gains possession and then checking back quickly toward the ball to collect a pass to feet.

- *Dribbling:* Wide attackers who have the ability to dribble and beat opponents 1v1 are invaluable to a team and can destroy any defensive system or tactic.

- *Receiving, turning, and playing one touch on the wing:* Wide attackers who possess tight ball control and fluid receiving skills have the best chance to eliminate defenders and evade close marking. Receiving and turning to face the opponent is often the key to successful wide attacking. Once they're facing the opponent with the ball, any number of attacking options become possible, from going 1v1 on the dribble to combining with support players. Wide attackers often combine with their center forward or central midfield players to execute successful wall passes. If the wide attacker is marked tightly and cannot turn with the ball, one-touch play can often be used to break down the defense. Upon receiving the ball, the wide attacker uses a clever single touch of the ball to play it into the space either behind the fullback (down the line) or across the defender toward the inside of the field. This subtle one-touch move can create enough space for the wide attacker to retain possession and eliminate the tight marking defender.

- *Rotation:* Rotation is coordinated movement among teammates with the object of getting someone free from his markers in order to receive the ball. Rotation is an interchange (rotating) of positions between forwards, midfielders, or defenders. Rotation on the wing commonly involves an interchange between the wide attacker and the fullback. Rotation between the wide attacker and fullback often takes place as the play is building up from the back third and the near-side center back gains possession. As the center back receives the ball and controls it, the wide attacker makes a checking run in toward the center while the fullback makes a run straight up the wing. Another common rotation that takes place on the wing is between the wide attacker and central midfield player on the wide attacker's side. With the center back in possession, the wide attacker makes a checking run toward the center of the field while the central midfield player interchanges with the wide attacker and runs to the wing position.

Squad Crossing and Finishing

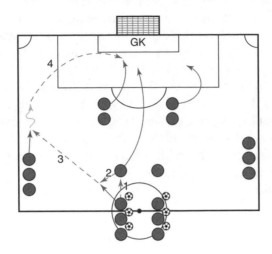

Purpose

Practicing the techniques, tactics, and movements needed for effective crossing and finishing

Organization

Set up play on half of a standard field. There are three wide attackers on each wing (left-footed players on the left and right-footed players on the right), two sets of two forwards at the top of the penalty area, and two lines of players near the center circle with one player positioned about 10 yards (9 m) away and facing her lines (midfield player).

Procedure

1. The server starts play by passing a ball to the midfield player facing her, who lays the ball off for the server to pass to the wide player on her side of the field.

2. After laying off the ball, the midfield player joins the runners in the box to receive the cross from the wide player.

3. The server becomes the next midfield player.

4. Players return to their same lines until changed by the coach.

Key Points

- The server and midfield player combine accurately to set up the through pass to the wing.
- Use proper weight, angle, and accuracy of the through pass to the wide attacker.
- The wide attacker should use good receiving skills and set up the ball for the cross.
- Make quality crosses into the penalty area.
- Use proper timing and angles of the three runs in the penalty box to finish the cross.

Variations

- The midfield player lays the ball back toward the inside (toward the far-side wing) and the server drives a long diagonal pass to the wide attacker of the far-side wing.
- Add goal-line servers who play extra balls in after the cross has been met so more than one player gets an attempt on goal after making a run in the penalty box.
- Have the two forwards work crossover runs in the box for variety.
- Allow the far-side wide attacker to make a run into the far-post area to add a fourth runner in the penalty box.

Three-Player Overlap Pattern

Purpose

Coordinating the passing and runs of three players working on an overlap pattern that includes a cross and finish on goal

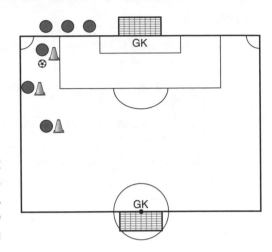

Organization

Set up half of a standard field with a portable goal at the half line. Set up three cones on each wing as shown for player start positions. There are two groups of three players each and a goalkeeper in each goal.

Procedure

1. Player A plays to player B (wide attacker).
2. Player B gathers the ball and dribbles inside toward player C (center forward), who is positioned on the edge of the penalty area.
3. Player A overlaps player B and collects a layoff pass from player C.
4. Player A takes the ball down the line and looks to cross to either player B or C, who are both making runs into the penalty area.
5. Players then go behind the goal, rotate positions, and work the same pattern back up the field in the other direction.

Key Points

- Start with a quality pass properly weighted on a good angle so the wide attacker can receive the ball, drive inside, and connect with the target player.
- The target player must create a good angle to receive the ball so that a quality pass can be played into the path of the overlapping player. The players in the box adjust the angle and timing of their runs to the overlapping player's approach to cross the ball.

Variations

- Add servers with extra balls along the goal line and have them serve a second ball to the runner who did not meet the first cross.
- Place a stationary player at the far post who is in position to finish a cross that arrives at the far post past the other two runners.

Two-Direction Finishing

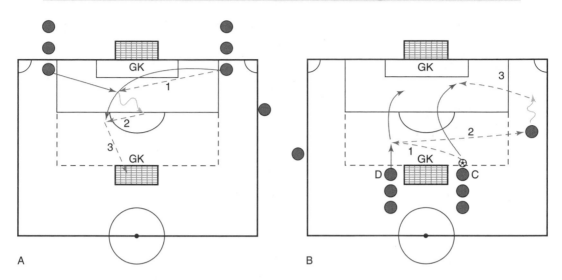

A

B

Purpose

Working overlap movements with a shot in one direction and then crossing and finishing in the other direction

Organization

Set up an area that is double the size of a standard penalty box, with a portable goal 36 yards (33 m) from the goal line. Players are in pairs and are positioned at each end on either side of the goals. One partner has a ball. There are also two side players positioned just outside the penalty area.

Procedure

Pairs of players work in opposite directions as follows.

End Line to Half Line (Diagram A)

1. Player A plays the ball to player B, who dribbles toward the middle.
2. Player A overlaps and receives a return pass into space for a shot on goal.
3. After the shot on goal, the partners join the ends of the lines to the sides of the goal they just attacked.

Half Line to End Line (Diagram B)

1. Player C passes to player D.
2. Player D passes to a wide player positioned outside the penalty area (alternate passing to both left- and right-side wide players)
3. Players C and D make near- and far-post runs to finish the cross.
4. After finishing the cross, the partners join the ends of the lines to the sides of the goal they just attacked.

Play continues in each direction alternately, with each pair working both finishing movements alternately.

Key Points

- The first pass and the overlapping moment should be executed at game speed and accuracy.
- The nonshooting player should follow in for a possible rebound shot.
- The weight and accuracy of the first two passes of the cross and finish are critical to set the pace of the drill.
- The wide attacker's first touch should set up the cross.
- The timing of the cross and the angle of the runs from the two central players must be in sync.

Variations

- Add servers with extra balls on each goal line to provide a pass for a finishing opportunity for the player who did not shoot or meet the cross.
- Allow the wide player who did not receive the pass to cross to make a run to the back post, joining the two central runners to finish on goal.

Final-Third Crossing and Running

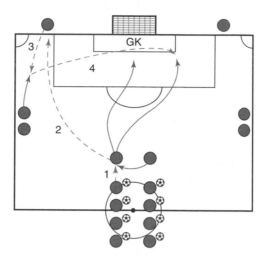

Purpose

Crossing the ball and making coordinated runs from midfield into the penalty box to finish

Organization

Set up play on half of a standard field with two lines of players near the center circle and another player (midfielder) facing each line 10 yards (9 m) away. Three wide attackers are positioned on each wing, with one of the three positioned as a target player on the goal line (left-footed players on the left and right-footed players on the right). A goalkeeper is in the goal.

Procedure

1. The first player in one line passes the ball to the midfield player facing him.

2. The midfielder stops the ball on the spot to set it up for the other midfielder, who comes across and passes it long down the wing to a target player.

3. The target player controls the ball quickly or lays it back first time toward the wide attacker, who is approaching in an attempt to cross the ball with one touch.

4. The two midfield players make runs into the penalty box to finish the cross.

5. The first players in each line move up to become the new midfielders, wide players rotate so there are two new target players at the goal line, and the original midfielders take their place at the end of their lines.

6. The next repetition uses the same sequence but to the other side.

Key Points

- The servers and midfield players combine accurately to set up the long through pass down the wing.
- The long pass to the goal-line target player must be played with the proper weight and angle.
- The wide player takes a position that best facilitates striking the cross with one touch.
- The runners in the box set the angle and timing of their runs to when the cross will be struck.

Variations

- Add servers with extra balls on the goal line to provide a pass for a finishing opportunity for the player who did not meet the cross.
- Add a stationary attacker at the far post on each side and have him attack the cross if it arrives in that area.
- Have the far-side wide attacker make a run into the box to add another runner to finish the cross.

8v8 Wingers Game

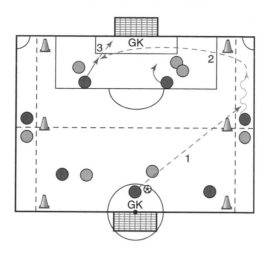

Purpose

Focusing on the skills and tactics of the wide attackers along with the coordination of crossing and finishing

Organization

Set up play on half of a standard field, placing a portable goal at the half line and marking a half line in the playing area. Two designated wing channels set up in the areas wide of the penalty box 18-yard (16 m) lines, as shown. There are two teams of seven players (three players in their defensive half, two players in their attacking half, and a wide player in each wing channel) plus a goalkeeper.

Procedure

Play two time periods as follows.

First Period (5 Minutes)

1. Ball is played directly to a wide attacker from any player.
2. The wide player has three touches to control and pass or cross.
3. When one winger is crossing the ball, the opposite winger is allowed to come out of the channel and attack the far post to add another runner in the box.
4. One of the three back players is allowed to cross the half and join the attack when one of the wingers is in possession so as to add another runner in the box.

Second Period (5 Minutes)

1. The ball must be touched by either of the two forwards before it can be played out to a wide attacker.

2. When one winger is crossing the ball, the opposite winger is allowed to come out of the channel and attack the far post to add another runner in the box.

3. One of the three back players is allowed to cross the half and join the attack when one of the wingers is in possession so as to add another runner in the box.

Key Points

- The team in possession should set up good spacing and support when playing out from the back, including when using the goalkeeper.

- Stress early crosses into the space behind the opponent's center backs with aggressive runs into near, midgoal, and far-post areas.

- Emphasize making an effort to get a minimum of three and hopefully four runners in the box to outnumber the defense on attacking the cross.

- The pace and trajectory of the cross is vital, as is making runs across defenders, to give attackers the best chance to make first contact on the ball.

Variations

- Eliminate the half line and play 8v8 with just the wing channels.

- Switch the wingers' positioning to have them play in the defending half of the channel, thus forcing them to cross the ball into the penalty area from a much deeper position (early cross).

- Eliminate the half line and wing channels and play 8v8 in the entire half-field area with emphasis on attacking from the flanks.

Free-Wing Crossing Boxes

Purpose

Playing a normal game while allowing players the opportunity to cross a ball unchallenged once they enter a key delivery area

Organization

Set up play on half of a standard field plus 18 yards (16 m), as shown. Set up a portable goal on this line. Mark four 15- × 10-yard (14 × 9 m) boxes on the wings as shown. There are two teams of eight players plus two goalkeepers.

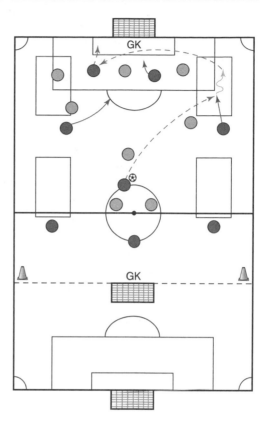

Procedure

1. Follow normal game rules with the following exception: Once a player gains entry into any of the four boxes with the ball, she cannot be challenged or tackled.

2. The player with possession inside a box must show urgency to cross the ball quickly (three touches or 3 total seconds).

3. Failure to cross the ball quickly at a normal game tempo results in a free kick for the opposition.

4. Any player can pass through the wing boxes in the run of the play without possession.

Key Points

- Encourage awareness and vision to get players into the wing boxes with passes or opportunities to dribble into the free areas.
- Once a team has gotten a player into the wing box, the other players must quickly get into the vital attacking areas to receive the cross.
- The quality of the cross is vital.

Variation

Play 11v11 on a full field with two full teams and adjust the wing boxes accordingly.

Functional Flank Play

Purpose

Emphasizing position-specific training for the role and function of the wide attacker in a gamelike setting

Organization

On the right side of a standard field, set up a training grid 40 yards wide × 70 yards long (37 × 64 m) which includes an area that extends 10 yards (9 m) beyond the half line. A 6-yard (5 m) target end zone runs the width of the field on the end without the goal. There are two teams of seven players, including a goalkeeper.

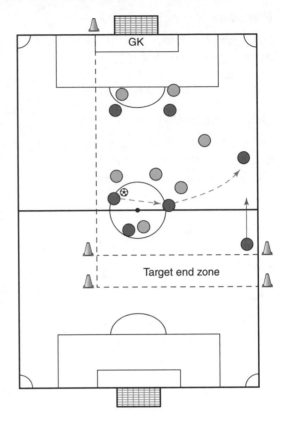

Procedure

1. Start play with the central midfield player in possession and the defending team moving into realistic positions based on the location of the ball.

2. The ball is played to the second central midfield player, who plays out quickly to the wide attacker.

3. A normal game ensues (normal offside rule applies), and the role and function of the wide player is highlighted by finding situations in the normal flow of a game that can involve the wide attacker.

4. Defense scores a point by getting the ball into the end zone under control.

5. Offense scores 3 points for a goal scored on the large goal.

Key Points

- Emphasize the wide attacker's skill to receive a pass under pressure and create combination play to eliminate defenders.
- The wide attacker must get into good crossing positions.
- A quality cross must be delivered into the penalty area.
- The players must coordinate their runs so they can attack the cross for a quality finish.
- The attacking players should be mindful of their defensive shape while attacking in order to prevent counterattacks.

Variations

- Start play with the goalkeeper where the team attacking the goal has to defend first and win possession. From the regain, see if the players can exploit the wing space and get the wide attacker on the ball.
- Set up the same area on the left side of the field and practice with the left-side wide attacker.

9v9 Flank Attacks

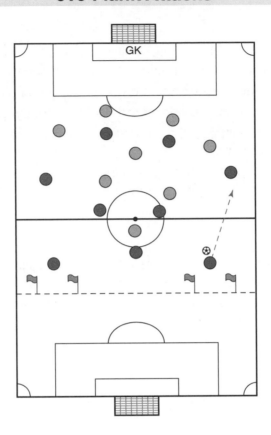

Purpose

Emphasizing position-specific training for both wide attackers in a game setting with normal rules

Organization

Set up an area that is half of a standard field plus 20 yards (18 m), as shown. Set up two target gates on the end line opposite the goal. There are two teams of nine players each, including the goalkeeper. The defending team plays in a 4-3-1+GK formation and the attacking team plays in a 3-4-2 formation.

Procedure

1. Start play with one of the attacking defenders in possession. They can play the ball wide and support play.
2. A normal game ensues (offside rule applies), and the role of the wide players on attack and defense is highlighted by looking for situations in the normal flow of a game to get the ball wide and attack from the flanks.
3. The defending players score a point by passing the ball through either gate once they cross the half line.

Key Points

- The game should focus on the movement of the wide attacker on the ball side to receive the ball and eliminate defenders alone or with combination play.
- If play is closed down to one side, see if the attacking team can switch the play and find the far-side winger.
- The wide player is encouraged to serve quality early or deep crosses into the penalty area.
- The far-side winger makes runs to the far-post area for the anticipated cross from the other side of the field.
- The team in possession must maintain a defensive shape while attacking in order to prevent a counterattack.

Variation

Play 11v11 with two full teams. Both teams focus on implementing the individual and team tactics relevant for attacking from the flanks.

8

Specialty Skills: Crossing and Attack Heading

Ian Barker

There is no such thing as a bad goal from the attacking team's point of view. That said, of the hundreds of ways goals can be scored, few are as stirring and memorable as the ones that result from a cleanly hit cross and a towering header.

As specialty skills, crossing and attack heading can be trained effectively through activity that is structured to allow for realism and frequency and that is developmentally appropriate for the age and level of the player. Players need deliberate practice, and they need consistent and timely feedback on their performance. It is important that skills are not trained in isolation beyond the fundamental stage of training. Placing players in their functional areas is necessary, as is progressively including opponents in activities. Crosses must come from a variety of areas in the wide space and with a variety of technical executions. At the same time, the type of attacking header should be varied, and if the cross cannot be met with the head, a finish should still be encouraged.

Both the men's and women's U.S. national teams have been fortunate enough to have world-class exponents of attacking heading. Brian McBride, holder of 96 international caps and 30 international goals, was a world-class header of the ball throughout his 16-year career, and his proficiency in the area allowed him to play professionally at the highest levels in the United States, England, and Germany. With more than 200 caps and 160 goals, Abby Wambach is perhaps the most dominant aerial threat in the world of women's soccer and has trained exclusively in the United States. Both McBride and Wambach owe a lot of their efficiency, however, to names such as Beasley, Sanneh, Donovan, Rapinoe, O'Hara, and Heath. In short, converters such as McBride and Wambach need service to convert, and so the skills of crossing and attack heading are linked. To emphasize this point with an example from the EPL in 2013, consider that Reading crossed the ball more than any EPL team and yet was relegated. This fact could be due to the lack of strikers to meet these crosses or the quality of the delivery.

As it was, Chelsea led the 2013 EPL in headed goals through services from names such as Juan Mata, Eden Hazard, and Oscar.

Without a doubt, stylistic and tactical approaches to the game put certain skills and proficiencies in the spotlight and others in the shadow. The influence of the Barcelona and Spain teams in promoting a possession-oriented game that seeks to play the incisive pass on the ground for the final strike at goal and attack zone 14 (the 25×20 yd [23×18 m] space centered just outside the penalty area) has led to the decline of wingers in many teams. Also, the development of formations such as 1-4-2-3-1 has narrowed team shapes at the expense of the winger. For Barcelona and Spain both, if a cross is to be made, it often will come from the wide defender or fullback, and the tactic of playing with the false nine (withdrawn forward) has discouraged services that are played to be attacked in the air.

Of the international confederations managing the game at an international level, the Union of European Football Associations (UEFA) is widely considered to be the most advanced in coaching education and game analysis. The UEFA website, www.uefa.com, is a valuable source of coaching information. In particular, the technical reports from UEFA club and international competition are rich with content. (UEFA authors technical reports for its major youth and senior competitions for men, boys, women, and girls.) A common theme in these technical reports is the state of wide play and the conversion of chances that come from wide play, specifically the head. UEFA reported that in the 2011 U17 and U19 male European championships, no goals were scored with the head. The report attributed this fact largely to a shifting emphasis on short passing, formation tendencies that sacrifice width for depth, and a fundamental lack of the skill of heading toward goal. UEFA's fears were allayed somewhat in 2012 when the U19 tournament produced 7 headed goals and the senior European Championships produced 22 headed goals. The fact, however, that UEFA is on notice as to how stylistic and tactical approaches affect certain skill sets merits attention.

There is a school of thought that the responsibility of the attacking header is to get to the right place and the responsibility of the crosser is to drop the ball into the right areas. At higher levels, it is true that the crosser has limited time to pick out the runners and the runners have limited time to assess the potential nature of the service. Because of this, the work on the training ground becomes essential for players to understand the tendencies of their teammates. Unlike the set play, with its clearly prescribed action and time to communicate that action, the cross in the run of play and the resulting attempt at goal require well-practiced understandings of players and game situations to be successful. The wide player who delivers primarily to a lone striker must be more specific about the areas targeted compared with the winger who delivers to twin strikers, perhaps even supported by a free-running midfielder.

Forwards will attack certain areas of the goal for many reasons. These may include their physical prowess, the runs of teammates, the positioning of opponents, the approach of the crosser to the ball, or simply a hunch.

A run to the near post is best timed to get across the goalkeeper at the same time the ball reaches that spot. If inside the goal frame, the forward can simply redirect the cross for a good scoring chance. If the forward's run takes him beyond the near post, the contact on the ball may be more glancing, trying to redirect it across the goal or back into play for support players. Failure to get across the goalkeeper makes for an easy save and will drive a coach to distraction.

A far-post run is effective for a number of reasons: It allows the forward more time to assess the flight of the ball, it provides a large attacking area at which to aim a header, and it causes defenders to split their attention between the ball and the run. If the ball is out-swinging and has made it to the far post, it is challenging to meet it with power and direction. Typically the forwards who are best at attacking the ball at the far post have size, power, and exceptional timing. Even at the highest levels, the attacking header at the far post is often best executed by keeping the ball alive and dropping back into the danger area.

A forward attacking the penalty spot or slot area on a cross is often brave, committing to meeting the ball with his head in a high-traffic zone and showing similar enthusiasm to surprise the opponent as the near-post runner. Attacking this area of the opponent's box often requires diving in front of a boot or a goalkeeper's punch. One exponent of this type of skill is Tim Cahill of Australian team Millwall, then Everton, and now the New York Red Bulls. Watching Cahill on television, and better yet live, it becomes readily apparent that he is blessed with bravery, technical skill, outstanding leaping ability, and great timing.

Crossers at the highest level are not content to merely deliver the ball into the attacking area. The effective crosser will practice in order to avoid some of the cardinal sins of the crossing. Among those sins are failing to serve the ball past the first defender, playing the ball too close to the goal-keeper, and hanging the ball up in such a way that it helps the goalkeeper and makes it impossible to meet the ball with power.

The ball that is cut back or driven to a trailing attacker is difficult to deal with if the defenders are moving into recovery positions. Though such a cross is seldom met with the head, it is an option that becomes possible when other runners are getting into areas looking for a cross to head. An effective crosser may set up the cutback by first serving several balls into the areas closer to goal.

Out-swinging crosses come back to the forward, and if they have enough pace and shape, they are inviting to attack. The in-swinging cross moves away from the forward, and if it is to be met with the head, it will typically be met by the diving header. Wide players such as Arjen Robben, who often play on the flank opposite of their dominant foot, seldom deliver crosses for headed attempts at goal unless they deliver with the less dominant foot. Instead, such players will cut in for a shot at goal, dribble to the end line, and cut the back ball back or in-swing the ball for a finish that is seldom delivered with the head. As such, the service that most often results in a headed strike at goal is an out-swinging one.

As we move to consider some activities to train the specialty skills of crossing and attack heading, the following points stand out: Goals scored from a cross and a header greatly entertain the fans. These skills need to be practiced in ways that allow for frequency and realism if they are to be perfected in competition. The U.S. national teams have presented excellent exponents of these skills to international soccer. These skills will always be important regardless of current trends within the game. They are inter-dependent and should be trained together beyond the most fundamental stage. Effective crossing and attack heading can take many forms based on players' technical and physical abilities as well as their tactical awareness of game situations.

Attacking-Head Tennis

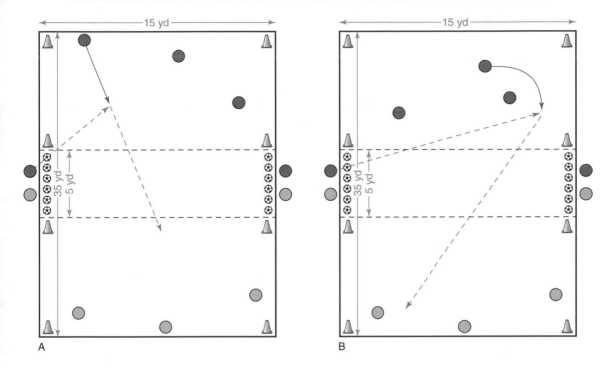

A

B

Purpose

Getting players comfortable attacking the ball with their head as well as considering where they head the ball and the shape of their approach to the ball relative to the service and the direction they intend to head it

Organization

Set up a playing area that is 35 × 15 yards (32 × 14 m) with a 5-yard (5 m) neutral zone. There are two teams of three players each who position in their halves of the area as shown. Each team has a server on either side of the neutral zone with a supply of balls. Use flags to mark the corners of the area.

Procedure

1. A server delivers the ball by hand to teammates who head at the opposing team's end line.

2. If the ball crosses the end line below the height of the flag, a goal is scored.

3. The opponents must control the ball without using their hands and keep the ball in their area. Then the service goes to them.

4. If the ball can be headed back for a score from an opposing attacking header, a double goal is scored.

5. Service and runs can vary. For example, in diagram A, the player runs in a straight line to meet the ball and directs it where he is moving.

In diagram B, the player makes a bent run to the ball as the ball is in flight longer and redirects it toward the end line.

Key Points

- The primary objective of the activity is to give the players a lot of opportunities to head the ball in an attacking manner with direction and power. Frequency is ensured and the players develop comfort based on the speed and strength of the delivery.

- The fundamentals of meeting the ball with the forehead with eyes open and heading the ball down can be repeated and immediate feedback given.

Variations

- Have the service come from a half or full volley.

- Decrease the attacking target area (height of the goal and width of the end line).

- Increase the length of the attacking space.

One-Touch Crossing

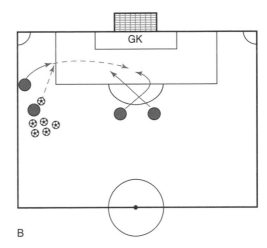

A   B

Purpose

Giving players repetition in crossing the ball with a variety of crossing techniques and approaches to the ball

Organization

Set up an area on half of a standard field. The activity is conducted to one full goal with a goalkeeper and two forwards attacking the goal. In the wing space, pairs of players act as server (S) and crosser (C).

Procedure

1. Play starts on a wing space by a player playing the ball forward for his partner to cross the ball to the two forwards for an attempt to score. After an attempt on goal, the forwards reset to their starting positions and play starts from the opposite wing space.

2. Crosses can vary. For example, in diagram A, the ball is played straight ahead of the crosser, who has one touch. With no time to adjust his run, the cross will need to be clipped or driven into the box. In diagram B, the ball is angled infield. Though the crosser has one touch, he can shape his run to come around the ball and create loft and curve.

Key Points

- The primary objective of the activity is to give the players a lot of opportunities to cross the ball.
- Frequency is ensured and the players develop awareness of the type of service dictated by their approach to the ball.
- Fundamentals such as where on the ball to make contact, how to impart spin, and how to drive the ball can be repeated and immediate feedback given.

Variations

- Increase the pace of the service to the crosser.
- Give the crosser a second touch.
- Identify specific areas for the crosser to serve the ball to.
- Identify specific types of delivery for the crosser to serve.

Near, Far, and Slot Movement

Purpose

Allowing for frequent service and movement into attacking space; a fundamental activity with significant teaching and learning opportunities

Organization

This activity requires a full-size goal and half a field with the 18-yard (16 m) box marked out. There are three forwards (additional forwards keep the activity flowing), two wide players, and an opposing goalkeeper. Cones can be used to help forwards with the shape of their runs and to serve as the offside line to help forwards with timing.

Procedure

1. One wide player serves to the other, who serves into the area as quickly as possible.

2. The three forwards must identify three attacking spaces: near post (N), far post (F), and the slot (S), approximately the penalty spot. The activity has three primary service areas: the byline (see diagram A), a space 18 to 25 yards (16-23 m) upfield (see diagram B), and a space just over the halfway line (see diagram C).

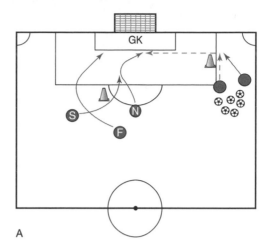

A

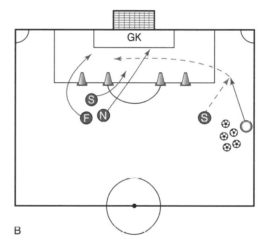

B

C

Key Points

- The timing of the forwards' runs is important.
- Players must communicate runs to teammates.
- Players must adjust movement to the delivery of the ball.

Variations

- Have crosses from both flanks.
- Add defenders.
- Remove the cones that shape the runs.
- Ask the wide players to mix up the timing of the service, requiring the forwards to recycle their runs.
- Add pressure on the cross.

Functional Crossing and Finishing

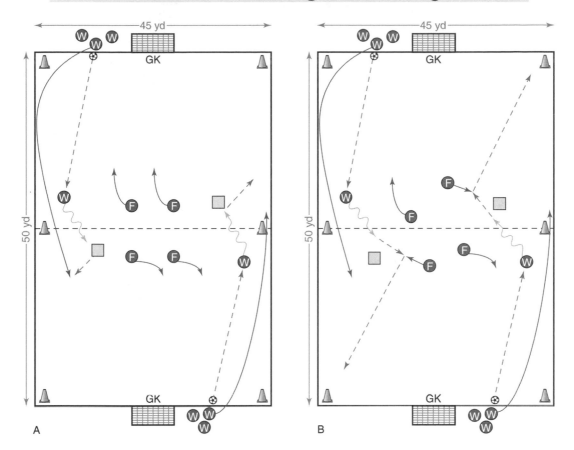

A

B

Purpose

Providing realistic, frequent crossing and finishing opportunities

Organization

Set up a 40- × 50-yard (37 × 46 m) playing area with two full-size goals at each end. There are at least eight wide players, four strikers, two mannequin defensive players, and a goalkeeper for each large goal.

Procedure

1. Two wide players set up a crossing opportunity for two strikers to attack by creating a two-player overlap. The deep wide player plays the ball to the advanced wide player, who attacks inside the mannequin defensive player and then plays the ball wide to the overlapping player, who then crosses the ball to the forwards. See diagram A.

2. After the cross, the overlapping player becomes the advanced wide player. The first advanced player rotates to the other side. This is repeated on both sides of the field. The wide players circulate through

the activity toward both goals. Crossing opportunities are created by two wide players plus a striker. See diagram B.

3. The deep wide player passes the ball to the advanced wide player, who receives the ball and dribbles toward the center, allowing time for the deep player to overlap. The ball is then played to a checking striker, who passes the ball to the overlapping wide player. The striker then quickly gets to a position in relation to the other forward to receive the cross.

Key Points

- Make frequent services into key areas.
- Timing of the strikers' runs in relation to the service is a key.

Variations

- Add some defenders to support the goalkeeper.
- Set the activity for right-footed service and then switch to left-footed service.

Phase of Play

Purpose

Establishing patterns of play to spring players in wide space to deliver to multiple attacking options

Organization

Set up a 75- × 70-yard (69 × 64 m) playing area with a full-size goal at one end and counterattack goals for the team defending the full goal. One team has a goalkeeper and seven field players arranged 3-3-1. The other team has eight field players arranged 2-4-2.

Procedure

1. The activity begins with the team attacking the full goal in possession.
2. With one additional field player and a formation that encourages width, the team attacking the full goal must try to find their most unmarked player, who should be wide.
3. If the opponent overplays defending the wide space, then going directly to goal is encouraged.
4. The team defending the full goal counters to the small goals.

Key Points

- Encourage the attacking team to work the ball and move the opposing defenders in order to spring a teammate in the wide space.
- When the ball is wide and the cross is to be delivered, the runs of the twin forwards, the weak-side wide player, and the central midfielders are important.

Variations

- Prescribe some patterns of play to the attacking team.
- The center back (CB) plays to the forward, who drops to the center midfielder (CM), who plays into the wide player (see diagram).
- The ball is played into the center midfielder, who drops to the center back, who plays the ball to the wide player.
- The ball is played into the wide player, who immediately attacks 1v1.
- The ball is played into the wide player, who initiates a switch of the point of attack through the central players to the wide player on the other flank.

Attacking Corners Game

Purpose

Rewarding the team that can get into the advanced wide space of the opponent, allowing for a cross or dribbling penetration along the goal line

Organization

Set up a 75- × 55-yard (69 × 50 m) playing area with two full-size goals at each end. In each corner, a 5- × 5-yard (5 × 5 m) triangle is marked out. There are two teams of seven players each.

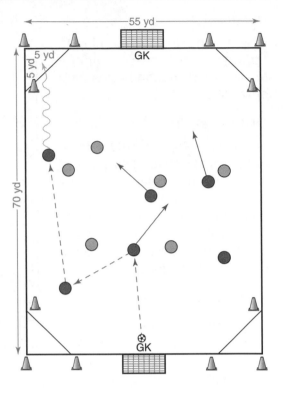

Procedure

1. The activity is played as a regular 7v7 game.

2. If a team can penetrate by a pass or on the dribble into the corner area, they cannot be immediately challenged, allowing for a cross occurring from behind the opponent or a penetrating dribble along the goal line for a potential cutback.

Key Points

- Encourage the attacking team to get the ball into wide advanced spaces and get behind the opponents.
- The opponents are now challenged to deal with the cross or penetrating dribble and track runners off the ball.

Variations

- Require playing into the corner area before going to goal.
- Penetration into the corner can occur only by a pass or a dribble.
- A defender can challenge in the corner area once the ball has been collected.

Attacking Wing Game

Purpose

Emphasizing game conditions with some small tweaks to encourage crossing situations

Organization

Set up a 70- × 50-yard (64 × 46 m) playing area with two full-size goals at each end and 5-yard (5 m) wing spaces that extend beyond the playing area. There are two teams of seven players each.

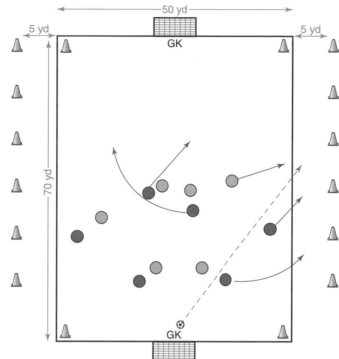

Procedure

1. The activity is played as a 7v7 game.

2. If an attacker goes into the wing space, he may be confronted by an opposing player to create a 1v1 wide.

3. If the 1v1 occurs, then a second attacker may join in to create a 2v1 opportunity wide.

Key Points

- Encourage the attacking team to go wide and incentivize this by allowing an overload to occur.

- When forwards see the ball go wide, they can then determine their attacking runs to meet the ball.

Variations

- The wide player receives the ball, is unchallenged, and can select his cross.

- The wide player is confronted and may take the opponent on 1v1 in the wide zone.

- The wide player receives support from behind and creates an overlap situation.

- The wide player receives support ahead and can play a penetrating ball in the wing zone.

9

Shooting and Finishing

Bobby Clark

What is the difference between shooting and finishing? Let's look at it this way—a player can shoot the ball well but may not necessarily be a good finisher. I was fortunate during my playing career to have played with some great finishers. I also played with some players who were hard shooters but not necessarily good finishers.

The first great finisher who springs to mind is Joey Harper. I first came across Joe when he was a 15-year-old playing for the Scottish U18 team in the UEFA youth championships in the Netherlands. Joe was the youngest on our squad, but because of his uncanny ability to put the ball in the net, he found his way onto the team. Later, I was lucky enough to team up with Joe when we were with Aberdeen, and in his time there, the 5-foot, 6-inch (168 cm) striker managed to score in excess of 200 goals. He scored goals at every level and in every club from his beginnings with Morton to his work for Aberdeen, Hibernian, and Everton. He had a wonderful ability to score goals.

The other player from my playing days now manages Liverpool and possibly is better known on the world stage. Yes, most soccer people are aware of Kenny Dalglish. I had the misfortune of playing against him during his Celtic days and the good fortune of playing and practicing with him in his Scotland days. Like Joe Harper, Kenny was not the fastest player, but he was very quick, and most of all, he was quick thinking. He always knew where the goal was, and in the penalty box when everything was busy and frantic, he had the calmest of temperaments. It almost looked as if the game came to a stop as he calmly slotted the ball into the back of the net.

I used the word *slot*. Sometimes Joe or Kenny would slot the ball into the net, but they could also hammer the ball home. Other times it was a pass, a curling shot, or a dipping volley. They both had a great repertoire of shots and seemed to have the ability to use the right weapon at the right time. This is the difference between shooting and finishing, and it is crucial that players learn finishing rather than just learning to shoot the ball hard. Don't get me wrong, there is a time for learning the proper techniques to shoot, bend, and dip the ball, but the most important thing is for players to experience gamelike situations where they learn the art of finishing.

I also have been fortunate enough to coach some terrific finishers here in the United States. Vladi Stanojevic still holds the Dartmouth career points record for the program, and Joseph Lapira scored 21 goals in his junior year at Notre Dame on his way to winning the 2006 Hermann Trophy. In fact, Notre Dame's strikers have led the Big East Conference players in scoring in 2006 (Joe Lapira), 2008 (Bright Dike), 2009 (Bright Dike), 2010 (Steven Perry), and 2012 (Ryan Finley). That's 5 out of 7 years.

We do few line drills, and most of the finishing drills we do are in game-like situations. I do, however, strongly encourage players to spend time after practice hitting a bag of balls. I always have a bag of balls handy so the players can take 10 minutes after practice or come down when they have some spare time and hit a bag of balls. During this time they can work on their technique and build confidence, but to score goals they also need to play the game and understand how to make space for their shot. Although good finishers are usually a little greedy, they do need to know how to combine with their teammates. They need to know how to find space, time runs, and get into good spots to get their shot off.

Having been a goalkeeper, I was always around finishing practices, trying to find out what makes strikers tick. I was studying their art while trying to thwart them. I had to understand their thinking, and this was possibly the best lesson I could have learned when I became a coach.

Every coaching session needs a beginning; an introduction. It is important for the coach to set the scene. You may discuss the aim of a session in the locker room, but the technical part of the warm-up is crucial. The session described in this chapter is one of my favorites and I use it a lot, especially in the winter and spring semesters, when I am teaching. I was first given the basic seeds of this session when I was coaching at Stanford. Tommy Wilson, who was one of the Scottish full-time staff coaches, brought the practice with him when he came to work at our summer camp. Tommy is now the reserve team coach with the Glasgow Rangers and was also the Scottish U20 coach when they participated in the U20 World Cup in Canada.

The session is split into the technical warm-up, the finishing phase, and the game phase, which puts the players in a game situation. Following the first three phases are various developments. Do not progress to the development phases until the players have a good feeling for the initial stage. *Festina lente*—"Hurry slowly"—is a good guide phrase!

Combination Play

Combination play is the quick exchange of passes to gain a tactical advantage. Near the goal the defensive team limits space and time to play. Defenders are drawn to the ball. Passing the ball quickly creates space and gaps in the opponent's defense.

Purpose

Preparing players technically and tactically

Organization

Set up a 44- × 40-yard (40 × 37 m) area (a double penalty area). There are four groups of three players, with one ball per group. The coach is positioned outside the grid with a supply of extra balls.

Procedure

The groups of three move freely around the space, making passes and using the entire space. The coach determines the combination pattern to be trained, as follows.

Checking In

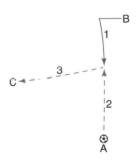

1. Players should practice checking in to receive the ball (player A to player B).
2. After player B has received the ball, he picks his head up and connects with player C.
3. Player C then connects with player A so that all the groups of three are moving freely around the area, playing passes.

Heel Takeover

1. Player A goes across the bows (dribbles across the intended path) of player B at right angles.
2. Player A stops the ball and moves on as player B moves off with the ball.
3. Player B can carry on to do a heel takeover with player C. This is simple, but timing and coordination are important. Player A can keep the ball and use player B as a decoy.

Straight Takeover

In the straight takeover, both players run toward one another. Some good coaching points are to emphasize both players accelerating out of the exchange and to encourage the player who has taken over the ball to take it in behind the other player using the outside of the foot.

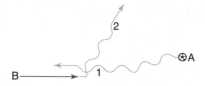

1. If player A carries the ball on his right foot, then player B will receive the ball on the outside of his right foot and take over the ball while reversing the direction.

2. As in the heel takeover, the player with the ball can retain the ball and use player B as a decoy. Player A, the player with the ball, controls this situation and determines whether he keeps the ball or makes the exchange.

Overlap

1. The overlap is when player A passes to player B, and as player B makes space, player A runs around her (overlaps) and player B plays the ball to the overlapping player A.

2. Player A then hits player C with a connecting pass.

3. The sequence begins again with player C doing an overlap around player A.

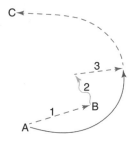

Round-the-Face Run

1. A round-the-face run is a run from the third player. Player A plays a pass to player B, who checks toward player C.

2. Player C times his run underneath player B and collects a pass from B. The pass can be first time but not necessarily, so the timing of the run is important.

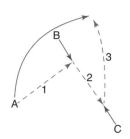

Key Points

- All groups are working freely and moving within the area as they make decisions about where and when to play. It is a busy but quiet activity where players practice skills that they will use later.
- There are a lot of short sprints in this warm-up, and I usually intersperse each exchange with a more static technical drill.
- It is important that the groups execute the combination plays in a realistic manner.
- The coach can train as many patterns in one session as is appropriate for the team.

Variations

- Adjust the size of the grid for a larger number of players.
- Change the speed of execution (e.g., 10 seconds at medium pace, 10 seconds at maximum speed).

Patterns

Patterns are a form of rehearsing a selection of passing combinations. The tactical combinations shown previously are trained at gamelike speed in the area of the field where it would happen, first without defensive opposition. The players on defense know your prime option is to go to goal for a chance to shoot. They are organized to deny time and space for the attackers to operate, so the technical and tactical execution must be near perfect. After adequate repetition, defensive opposition is added.

Serve—Collect—Run

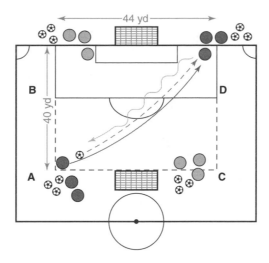

Purpose

Serving longer diagonal balls and running with the ball; warming up

Organization

Set up play in a 44- × 40-yard (40 × 37 m) area at one end of a standard field. Split 12 players so that 3 are at each of the four corners. Each player has a partner on the opposite diagonal. Players at corners A and D are on the same team and players at corners B and C are on the other team.

Procedure

1. Player A touches the ball and plays a diagonal pass to player D.
2. Player A then goes to D and D goes to A with the ball.
3. The same thing then happens for player B, who plays a long diagonal pass to player C and then moves to player C, who receives the ball and moves to B with the ball.

Key Points

- The player who begins the exercise must work on hitting a longer aerial pass, and the second player must work on receiving an aerial pass.
- Emphasize that the long pass should not be played from a stationary ball. Show the little setting-up touch that allows the head to come up and then the long pass. Making the players play a moving ball gets it looking like a game, not a set piece.

Purpose

Improving finishing and developing technique

Organization

Set up a 44- × 40-yard (40 × 37 m) area with balls at each corner. Split 12 players so that 3 are at each of the four corners. Each player has a partner on the opposite diagonal. Players at corners A and D are on the same team and players at corners B and C are on the other team. A goalkeeper is in each goal.

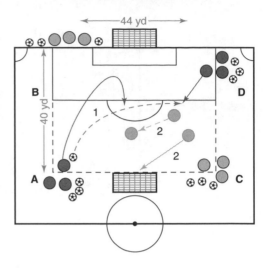

Procedure

1. Player A touches the ball and plays a diagonal pass to player D.

2. When the long pass is played from player A to player D, A must get out and perform an overlap or takeover with D before finishing with a shot on goal.

3. After the shot, the players switch places so that player A becomes player D and player D becomes player A.

4. The practice continues and the opposite now happens, with player B playing diagonal to player C. They do an exchange, take a shot, and then switch places.

Key Points

- Emphasize timing of the takeover or overlap and encourage a good shot on target.

- The player who does not hit the shot should be following up by looking for rebounds off the goalkeeper. (Some of the Joe Harper's best goals came from balls left on the doorstep.)

- At the beginning of the practice, don't worry too much about the score. Let players first learn the drill. Near the end of the practice, make it competitive; because there are two teams (As plus Ds and Bs plus Cs), it is easy to count the score. This gives the practice an edge and also teaches composure under pressure.

Service—2v1 to Goal

Purpose

Improving finishing, technical development, and individual attacking and defending

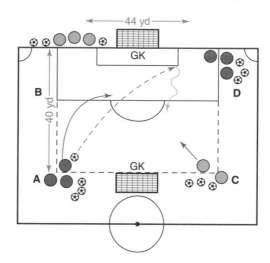

Organization

Set up a 44- × 40-yard (40 × 37 m) area with balls at each corner. Split 12 players so that 3 are at each of the four corners. Each player has a partner on the opposite diagonal. Players at corners A and D are on the same team and players at corners B and C are on the other team.

Procedure

This is similar to the previous drill (Service—Takeover or Overlap—Shoot) except that a player from corner C is now in the middle of the field as a defender. The sequence would look like this:

1. Player A plays over defender C to A's partner at D.
2. Player A then gets onside and plays a 2v1 situation against player C.
3. Once the sequence is over, the player who played the long pass (A) becomes the new defender and player D becomes an A. After the next sequence, the defender goes to D.

Key Points

- Look for combinations and mobility, and make sure the offside rule applies.
- Teach the attackers how to read the offside line and how to time their runs in behind the defense.
- The players are training their soccer minds while they are developing passing, dribbling, and finishing techniques.
- This is superb practice for the defenders because they need to know where to hold their line and when to drop.
- The defender should work on trying to isolate the player on the ball. (If this happens, perhaps it is the cue for an overlap.)
- If the defender wins the ball, he goes to the other goal and tries to score. This means that the As and the Ds are playing a game against the Bs and the Cs.
- After the skills have been bedded down, finish with the two teams counting score, and remember the offside rule is in operation. It is necessary to use the offside rule because the timing of the pass and the run are so important at the highest level.

Service—2v2 to Goal

Purpose

Improving finishing, technical development, and small group (2v2) attacking and defending

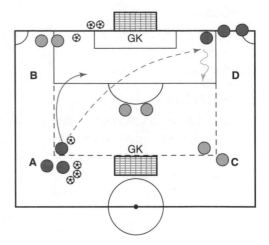

Organization

Set up a 44- × 40-yard (40 × 37 m) area with balls at each corner. Split 12 players so that 3 are at each of the four corners. Each player has a partner on the opposite diagonal. Players at corners A and D are on the same team and players at corners B and C are on the other team.

Procedure

1. Now there are two defenders and it becomes a 2v2 to goal.
2. Two defenders, B and C, are in the middle.
3. Player A plays the ball over the top to player D.
4. Player A then gets onside and plays with D in a 2v2 game against B and C.
5. If the defenders (B and C) win the ball, they go to the opposite goal.
6. After the sequence, A and B become the new defenders and play goes the opposite way.

Key Points

From the attacking perspective, these are the key points:

- The timing of runs is crucial.
- Communication and combining are continually happening, and players have to realize when they have created enough space to get off a shot.
- You do not need to beat an opponent to get off a shot.
- Sometimes you just make space and squeeze the ball past the defender. A good attacker often uses the defender as a screen.

From the defending perspective, these are the key points:

- It is about pressure and cover. Who presses the ball?
- Where and how does the first defender press the ball, and how does the second defender offer cover?

Again, once the players have a good feel for the practice, finish with both teams counting the goals. The players must experience the cutting edge of the game and have the cool head of a gunslinger. Both Joe Harper and Kenny Dalglish were the coolest players on the field even though they were in the penalty area, the hottest part of the field.

Service—3v2 to Goal

Purpose

Improving finishing, technical development, and small group (3v2) attacking and defending

Organization

Set up a 44- × 40-yard (40 × 37 m) area with balls at each corner. Split 12 players so that 3 are at each of the four corners. Each player has a partner on the opposite diagonal. Players at corners A and D are on the same team and players at corners B and C are on the other team.

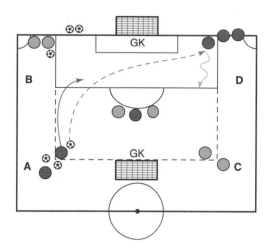

Procedure

1. Select a forward (F) from each team.
2. The forward comes on when her team is in possession, and the game now begins with two defenders and an opposing attacker in the middle.
3. When player A plays to player D, they then join with the forward and attack the two defenders in a 3v2 situation.

Key Points

- Teach players to look for third-man runs while still using takeovers and overlaps to create openings to get a shot off.
- The forward must learn how to play with her back to the goal or perhaps slide to wide areas.
- All players must be aware that they are in and around the goal and must always be looking for opportunities to shoot.
- There is a fine line between being goal greedy and passing up a good opportunity. Good goal scorers tend to lean toward the greedy side.
- Once again, it is important that the game finishes in competitive mode with both teams counting goals.

Team-Related Phases

The previous five phases involve everyone in the group playing both attacking and defending roles. This works well with a group of talented players. In the modern game, all 10 outfield players need to understand both attacking and defending concepts, and these activities teach everyone how to overlap and also how to prevent attacks. Having said this, I often structure the following practice a bit differently when I work with my team because I like to work players in their positions. The opposite diagonals (As plus Ds and Bs plus Cs) work together, but I take out two defenders from the As and Ds and two defenders from the Bs and Cs. Later in the progression I take out the forwards and then a recovering defender. I use several progressions to do this, as described next.

Position-Specific 2v2 to Goal

Purpose

Improving finishing, technical development, and small group (2v2) attacking and defending

Organization

Set up a 44- × 40-yard (40 × 37 m) area with balls at each corner. Split 12 players so that 3 are at each of the four corners. Each player has a partner on the opposite diagonal. Players at corners A and D are on the same team and players at corners B and C are on the other team. In addition, two sets of two defenders are positioned at the half line.

Procedure

1. Split the group on the diagonals, with the midfield players on the corners. The opposite diagonals are on the same team so that As and Ds are a unit and Bs and Cs are a unit.
2. Two sets of defenders come in from the half line.
3. If the drill begins with A playing the long diagonal to D, then the defenders out in the middle would be from the opposite team (Bs and Cs).
4. This sets up a 2v2 battle, with the midfield taking on the two defenders.

Key Points

- The attackers are trying to create space to get a shot and the defenders are trying to close down the attackers while also giving support to one another.
- If the defenders win the ball, they can counterattack, so this activity also teaches transitioning.
- There are good coaching moments both in attack and defense, but as always, I finish with a game where the goals are counted.

Position-Specific 3v2 to Goal

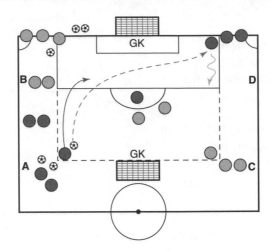

Purpose

Improving finishing, technical development, and small group (3v2) attacking and defending

Organization

Set up a 44- × 40-yard (40 × 37 m) area with balls at each corner. Split 12 players so that 3 are at each of the four corners. Each player has a partner on the opposite diagonal. Players at corners A and D are on the same team and players at corners B and C are on the other team.

Procedure

1. Similar to Service—3v2 to Goal, defenders are coming on as well as two forwards, one for each team.
2. The game starts with two defenders in the middle plus a forward from the opposing team.
3. When A plays the diagonal pass to D, they link up with the forward and play 3v2 against the two defenders. The defenders can counterattack.

Key Points

- This situation should produce scoring opportunities because the attackers have a man advantage.
- Teach the defenders how to defend when they're a man down, and if they win the ball and transition, they must attack quickly or they will soon be outnumbered.

Position-Specific 3v2 to Goal
With a Recovering Defender

Purpose

Improving finishing, technical development, and small group (3v2) attacking and defending

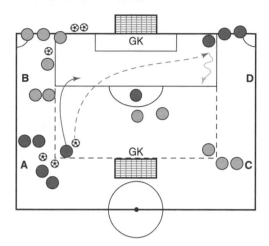

Organization

Set up a 44- × 40-yard (40 × 37 m) area with balls at each corner. Split 12 players so that 3 are at each of the four corners. Each player has a partner on the opposite diagonal. Players at corners A and D are on the same team and players at corners B and C are on the other team.

Procedure

1. Everything is the same as in Position-Specific 2v2 to Goal except there is a recovering player who can join the two defenders and make it 3v3.
2. Use fullbacks as the recovering players, because they are often recovering in a game after being up in an attack.
3. Player A hits a long diagonal to player D and joins him.
4. Both A and D plus the forward attack the two defenders.
5. After D receives the diagonal, the recovering defender then gets back and joins the two permanent defenders to make it 3v3.

Key Points

- This activity is very gamelike and the attackers have great opportunities to use combinations or individual skills to create openings for a finish on goal.
- The defense must work on pressuring the ball while offering cover and balance to the situation.
- This is really a mini game, with coaching points abounding. The team's defenders are getting great opportunities to defend and the midfield and forwards are working on combinations and finishing continually.

A technical warm up and eight practice phases have been described in this chapter. How do you put them all together? You certainly do not try to do them all in one go. Think about introducing them slowly throughout a season, adding a new bit after you feel that your squad has mastered the previous phase. Too much, too soon will confuse the players, and bewildered players are not in a good state of mind to learn.

The drip-feed method delivers the best results—give a little bit often and up the dosage at the correct time. After the technical warm-up, where you work on combinations, you might then start with the first phase, Combination Play. The next week you might add on phase 2, Serve—Collect—Run. Hurry slowly and watch carefully to determine how the players are progressing. If they need help or need to work on their finishing, stay at phase 1, or at least begin every practice here. This is an unopposed situation and gives the players plenty of practice doing the combinations and getting shots off. As this becomes natural, add more opposition. The 2v1 is a good progression. Once your players understand the concepts, you can move right through the various practices.

As I mentioned earlier, I like how this series of practices teaches finishing techniques in gamelike situations. I love the fact that there is an offside line, because this is so critical in the timing of runs. Do the forwards bend their run or do they fade out? Do they make runs from slightly deeper positions so they are moving in behind the defense at the right moment when the pass is delivered? Good forwards are always playing right on the last defender and know how to get in behind the opposing defense.

These practices are tremendous for working your defenders. Whether it is an even situation or a numbers-down situation, they need to know how to react. When will they pressure? Who will provide cover, and when you move to 3v3, what is their balance? I remember Roy Reece, a former U.S. U17 coach, making this statement during a lecture: "If you want to improve your attacking, work on your defending." If your defending is poor, then the attackers do not need to be very good to gain an advantage. If, however, your defending is strong, then your attackers also need to be strong if they are going to gain an advantage.

Corner Kicks and Throw-Ins

Thomas Durkin

The ultra-organized, compact defense is a growing feature of modern soccer teams. Closing off space and making it tougher to penetrate has made the vital-area goals harder and harder to come by from the run of play. Because there are so many players in one area of the field, the run of play is often interrupted by defensive challenges that send the ball out of touch or over the end line. Play has stopped, and the game changes from a free flow of passes to both teams quickly organizing for the ball to be put back into play. At these moments, there is a need for specialized plans to score directly or to help maintain possession and keep the attack alive. Tight games are often decided by teams that see these moments as opportunities and prepare for them. When the ball goes out of touch in the attacking half, a team can keep the heat on the opponents by maintaining possession or threatening to score directly from a throw-in. A foolish loss of possession in this area of the field wastes potential opportunities and can cause your entire team to make 40- to 50-yard (37-46 m) defensive recovery runs.

Corner Kicks

When the whistle sounds, the assistant referee points to the corner flag, the referee signals for a corner kick, and the defending team, although tough to get behind in free play, is forced to deal directly with a potential goal-scoring situation. For spectators and supporters, this stimulates a sense of excitement or impending doom. For the attacking team, there is a chance to put to the test the actions rehearsed on the training ground for just such a moment. Will it be the out-swinger driven toward the penalty spot for the attacker to meet while teasing the goalkeeper to come off the goal line, or will it be the in-swinger, tight to the end line and behind the defenders for the attackers to run onto? Will it be a lofted ball to the far post or a driven near-post ball? Will it perhaps be the short corner or some trick play that will penetrate the goal box? Whatever the choice of tactic, the situation requires a well-delivered pass to well-timed and organized runs into the goalmouth.

It is hard to ignore the statistical data. During the 2013 Major League Soccer (MLS) regular season, 845 goals were scored. Of these, 87 (10.35 percent) were scored directly from or within 15 seconds of a corner kick. From a total of 323 games, there were 241 wins and thus 241 game-winner goals. Thirty-four of these game winners were scored within 15 seconds of a corner kick (14.1 percent). Which team scored the most goals from corner-kick situations during the 2013 regular season? MLS finalist Real Salt Lake. How did Sporting Kansas City, the 2013 champion team, score to send the championship game into overtime? With a corner kick.

The four key aspects to note are

1. getting a moving player to meet a moving ball,
2. placing a premium on snapping up loose balls and deflections as a contingency plan,
3. instilling the will to fight for a rebound or faulty clearance in order to get a second chance at the prize, and
4. maintaining a balance by leaving enough players at the back of the team to ward off the opponent's counterattacks.

The focus of training for these situations is simple: Improve the odds of scoring goals while adding variety and resources to the arsenal. From the training ground, use the power of observation and intuition to decide which players to deploy in which roles to optimize success. Calculate the amount of risk by the number of players brought forward into the attack, the positions in the intermediate area for rebounds, and the number of players assigned to defend against a counterattack.

Player selection is the important first step. Foremost is the identification of one or two players who can deliver the ball from the corner mark to the designated areas in the box with the required trajectory and pace who may also be clever enough to pull off the short corner. Assign three or four players to attack the cross who are strong in the air by nature of their stature or leaping ability. Courage and aggressive attitude toward contact are also good attributes to look for. Find a poacher who has natural scoring instincts and quick reflexes to convert half chances and knockdowns or run interference in tight to the goal. Add a couple of players who strike the ball well from a distance or volley the ball from outside the goal box to deal with the initial clearance. Finally, position the remaining players to deal with the counterattack around the halfway line. A speedy player for cover and a strong marker make a good partnership at the back to deal with the counterattack.

My personal preference is always to start with the most immediate method of scoring, and that is a direct ball driven into the space in the box where the best header of the ball is most comfortable going. Establishing that as a premise from the right and left side, a variety of options can be layered in as one learns more about the team and the opponents.

The 1987 boys' team that I coached from U16 to U19 had a great cast of characters with a wide range of abilities around the goal. They were a great team whose ability to attack the goal was enhanced largely by their skill and prowess at set pieces. With two strong, tall athletic players in the center of the defense coming forward for corner kicks and restarts, it was almost a foregone conclusion that they would achieve a strike at goal. To see the opposing teams wince and shrink as these two came forward to take up their positions in the area just added to the team's confidence in these situations. With numerous possibilities for a great delivery of the ball from either side of the field and the constant threat of the short corner, our two big fellas enjoyed a great scoring record against all comers, from local league rivals to international opponents such as the Brazilian U17 national team. The team gained so much acclaim and confidence from these situations that they began to refer to the two players as *half a goal.*

After imprinting the general attacking and defensive shape for the team and outlining the style and system of play as they pertain to the principles of the game, the final step in game preparation is the basic nuts and bolts of how to attack and defend at restarts. Looking at the attacking corner kick as the primary example, we start with an orientation phase. In this segment, begin with only the principal characters involved. All you need is the main attackers and the opposing goalkeeper. Determine the type of corner the players prefer and allow the player taking the kick to establish the area of the goal box where he can deliver the ball accurately. It is important to strive for consistency in the serve.

Explore the various options for in-swinging and out-swinging crosses. Also, give simple signals for communication between the kicker and players in the box (e.g., hands on hips, hand in the air, two hands in the air).

The next task is to coordinate the runs to the type of service that has been signaled with the purpose of getting the first-choice header of the ball to the designated area. The complementing runs should cover the other dangerous spaces in front of the goal in case the cross falls short or long of the targeted zone, the runs are mistimed, or the service is subpar. The timing of the runs is a determining factor. Designating realistic starting positions for each player and then sequencing the runs helps ensure organization. It is good practice to have one player run early as a decoy to stir movement in the box and create space for others to run into. In addition, it is important for the attackers to be active at the start positions with feet moving and feinting actions to gain a step on their markers and a running start toward the ball.

A number of patterns and formations can be set up in the box, but the essential format is that all the players follow their routes from start to finish. Aggression and the desire to be first to the ball are the cornerstones of success. Running across the face of the opponent with a sudden burst of speed or ghosting off the opponent's back shoulder to get in behind him are important strategies to consider. Teach one or two attackers how to position outside the penalty area in order to deal with the clearances. Ask the goalkeeper to deliberately punch and box balls away for the sake of the exercise.

Following are some ideas for the organization and training of corner kicks. Keep in mind that players make plans successful. It is your task to select the right players and make them feel knowledgeable about and confident in their roles.

Orientation Phase for Corner Kicks

During the orientation phase of training, players are introduced to the tactical concepts to be trained. The players are placed in starting positions and practice specific patterns and options. The activities are trained in the specific area of the field pertinent to the tactics. In the beginning, there is no defensive opposition. As the players learn the patterns, they should execute them as close to game speed as possible. Later, the coach can add several defenders to create more gamelike training.

Corner-Kick Pressure the Keeper

Purpose

Putting the goalkeeper under pressure and forcing a loose ball

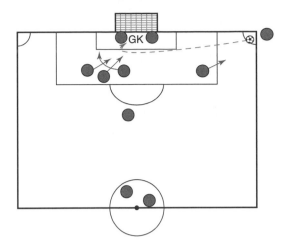

Organization

Set up play on half of a standard field. There are 11 players: 1 attacker in front the goalkeeper to impede his path to the ball, 1 player behind to further limit the mobility of the goalkeeper, 1 attacker for the short option, 3 players to cover the area of knockdowns at the back of the 6-yard (5 m) box and around the penalty spot, 1 player positioned outside the box, 2 players back, and an opposing goalkeeper.

Procedure

1. An in-swing ball is played as directly as possible to the goal area tight to the goal line.
2. The players closest to the goal use every legal means to disrupt the goalkeeper and attack the ball for a nod-on, flick, or chance at goal.
3. The other attackers place a premium on snapping up the second-chance balls.

Key Points

- Be careful not to foul the goalkeeper.
- Runs may have to be improvised, delayed, or recycled.
- Stay alert until the play is over.

Variations

- The ball can be played to either line.
- No exchange takes place.

Corner-Kick Inside Out

Purpose

Creating space in front of goal to attack the ball

Organization

Set up play on half of a standard field. There are 11 total players: 1 player on the ball, 6 players in the goal box, 1 player on top of the box, 2 players back, and an opposing goalkeeper.

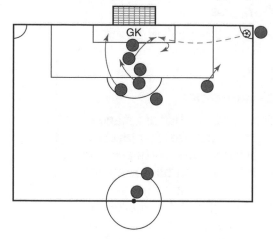

Procedure

1. An in-swinging cross is played to the area between the penalty mark and the 6-yard (5 m) box.
2. The players in the box line up into rows of three, with one player on the 18-yard (16 m) line.
3. The two lines of three players interchange while running screens on the markers. The exchange brings the farthest line toward the goal and the nearest away for rebounds and deflections.
4. The runner on the edge of the area attacks the space between the two lines.

Key Points

- Hit the in-swinging ball with pace to the area just on the edge of the 6-yard (5 m) box.
- The players should be active in the starting positions and make runs in unison.
- Both lines should strive for a screening action to slow down the markers and gain a step on them.

Variations

- The ball can be played to either line.
- No exchange takes place.

Rafa Corner Kick

Purpose

Catching the opponent off guard and creating a direct strike on goal

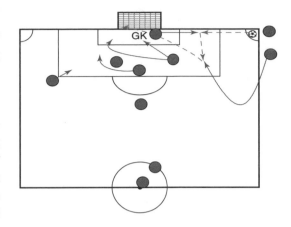

Organization

Set up play on half of a standard field. There are 11 players: 2 players over the ball, 1 player on the near post, 3 players in the box, 2 players outside the box, 2 players back, and an opposing goalkeeper.

Procedure

1. The two players over the ball argue over who will strike the ball. The decoy player walks away dejected.
2. The players in the box do a false start as the server approaches the ball.
3. The near-post runner dashes out for the short pass.
4. The decoy, having walked back toward his position, doubles back toward the area with a sudden acceleration.
5. The server plays the ball to the near-post runner low along the end line.
6. The near-post runner lays a soft pass into the path of the decoy.
7. The ball is shot hard and low to the far post.
8. The runners frame the goal at the far post in case of rebounds or deflection.

Key Points

- The acting at the corner flag must be convincing.
- You only get one chance at a trick play; the opponent won't be fooled twice.
- The timing of the movement of the three main players needs to be perfect.
- The pass and shot need to be on first-time actions.
- The runners need to cover the back post for balls going wide, rebounds, or deflections to help the ball over the goal line.

Learning Phase for Corner Kicks

For drills in the learning phase, opponents are added to increase pressure and complicate the environment. A well-positioned defender in the near-post zone, dealing only with the ball, is common in most defensive setups. Many times this is just enough pressure to put off the service to the box and affect the sight lines or timing of the runs. The addition of a defender to the near and far post requires a more accurate finish from the attackers. After reacquiring the sense of timing and delivery from both sides, introduce opponents to mark the runners. Start them off as a presence and gradually increase the resistance to full pressure. The action of the defending team is somewhat unpredictable, so encourage the attackers to improvise within reason and be creative with their choices. The players outside the box can still have a free go at goal but must make adjustments for the added traffic in front of them in order to get the ball on target. The runners need to stay alert and active until the play is over, and they may need to recycle the runs. Once a significant amount of success has been achieved, add an opponent to dispute the rebounded balls and help the clearance along. Finally, add enough opponents to create a counterattacking situation and organize the attacking team for countermeasures to maintain balance and safety.

Near and Far Corner Kick

Purpose

Developing coordination and timing for runs and service to the box and establishing signals for communication

Organization

Set up play on half of a standard field. There are 10 offensive players: 2 players to work out the in-swinging and out-swinging service from the corner arc, 4 to 5 players to cover the areas for runs in the box, 2 players positioned outside on the perimeter of the goal area, 3 defenders, and an opposing goalkeeper.

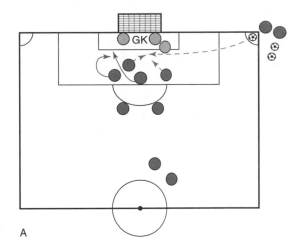

A

Procedure

1. Play starts with a corner kick.

2. Allow the servers frequent repetition of service from both the right side and left side of the pitch. Determine the best area for serving the ball that will be consistent.

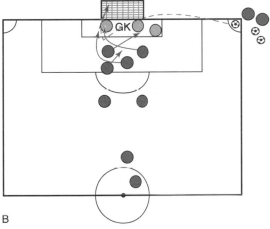

B

3. Develop a signal from the server for a near-post service (diagram A) and a far-post service (diagram B).

4. Work to coordinate, sequence, and time the runs in the box to the designated areas.

5. Address the quality of the cross pass and finishing action. Make sure that the players in and outside the goal box are ready for deflections, rebounds, and clearances.

Key Points

- Demand good delivery. It is good practice to over-hit the ball.
- Make sure that all the players run the full route to the designated areas.
- If it's difficult for the player to convert the cross, they should try to make it easy for someone else.

Variations

- Add five more opponents—one on each post and one at the front of the 6-yard (5 m) box. This will increase the difficulty for the servers and affect the timing of runs.

- Gradually work from passive to full pressure.

- If a serve goes in the goal area, have the keeper box the ball out (see diagram C). The offensive players should be in position to regain possession for a shot on goal.

- Try all types of corner kicks from both sides. If the defense gets possession, they try to complete 5 consecutive passes (see diagram D).

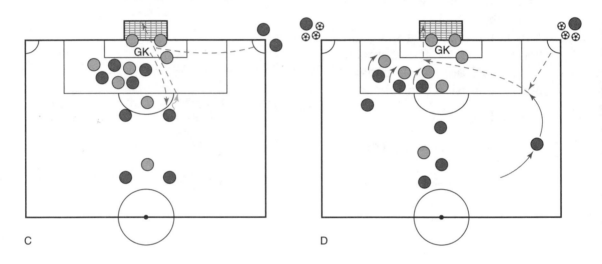

C

D

Corner-Kick Competition

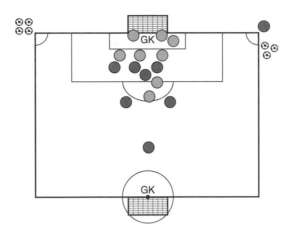

Purpose

Developing coordination and timing for runs and service under pressure from the opponent and improvising when necessary

Organization

Set up play on half of a standard field with a counterattacking small goal at the center of the midfield line. Place a supply of balls at each corner. There are eight attacking players and eight defensive players plus a goalkeeper. The defensive team is organized with a player on each post, a player zoning at the near post, and four players matching up against four attackers.

Procedure

1. Six corner kicks are taken from each corner.
2. Have the players work out which attacking corner kick they will play with the signals they have developed.
3. Try both the short and long options.
4. Allow adequate time to set up each play between reps.
5. An attempt is finished when the ball goes out of bounds or 10 seconds pass.

Points are awarded as follows. The attacking team scores 3 points for a goal directly from a corner kick or within 10 seconds and 1 point for an attempt on goal saved by the keeper within 10 seconds of a corner kick. The defending team scores 1 point for six consecutive passes after winning possession and 3 points for scoring in the counterattacking goal.

Key Points

- Be first to the ball. Outplay the marker by running free and be first to the designated area.
- Improvise if your path gets blocked or the service is not ideal.
- Use a big surface to convert the cross and try to get over the top of a ball and push it down toward the back of the net.
- Battle! Make sure the attackers are controlled yet aggressive.
- Pressure the ball immediately if possession is lost.
- Don't lose concentration; stay alert until the play is over.

Variations

- Give each team a chance to attack.
- Use different numbers for each team.

Orientation Phase for Throw-Ins

A throw-in in the attacking half of the field is an advantage and should be viewed as such. This simple restart is often overlooked as an opportunity to create an indirect threat at goal or establish settled possession in a forward position on the field. A direct threat is possible via the long throw-in, but I am more in favor of using it to add an element of surprise rather than as an attacking tactic.

The first order of business is for attackers to clear the area close to the thrower as a means of creating space. Far too often, teams and individuals make the mistake of positioning too close to the touchline, thereby consolidating the defense at the point of attack. This makes the thrower's job to complete a pass that much more difficult.

The thrower needs to deliver the ball in one smooth motion. As with any other pass, take into consideration the timing, weight, and trajectory of the pass for the desired outcome. The pass should screen the ball away from the marker, lead the teammate into open space, and be played to feet as often as possible except where a flick-on is in the design. The long throw is the simulation of a crossing action and requires a specialist. It can be set up similar to the organization of a corner kick. A well-placed ball to the near post or center of the area can be a difficult and unwelcome threat to opposing defenses; nerves alone may yield a chance.

After the throw-in, the thrower needs to reenter the field of play and quickly join up with the attack or buildup. Dividing the attacking half into two zones can give attackers insight as to the desired outcome of the throw-in. Close to the midfield stripe, the aim should be to establish possession of the ball in order to restart the buildup or change the point of attack. As the action gets closer to the end line, the priority shifts to the quick setup of a crossing or shooting action or getting the ball to a post-up player in the goal box for others to work off.

Following are some ideas for the organization and training of throw-ins. Keep in mind that players make plans successful. It is your task to select the right players and make them feel knowledgeable about and confident in their roles.

Throw-In Attack or Possession

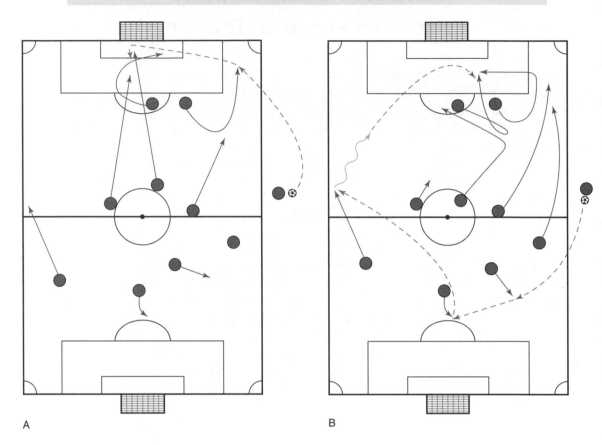

A

B

Purpose

Improving the ability to establish settled possession or an attacking move directly from a throw-in

Organization

Set up play on a standard field. Start with nine players on the field and one player in position to throw the ball in play.

Procedure

1. Determine the starting positions of the principal players and select a player to deliver the throw-in based on the team formation or any special attributes. Define the roles, assign the tasks to the principals, and work out the communication between the thrower and the rest of the team.

2. Define the objective of the exercise based on the position of the throw-in and the desired outcome (i.e., penetration as shown in diagram A or possession as shown in diagram B).

3. Once the players have rehearsed several patterns, they execute the patterns at game pace.

Key Points

- Keep the activity flowing to ensure many repetitions.
- Let the players choose any pattern. Encourage improvisation.

Learning Phase for Throw-Ins

For drills in the learning phase, opponents are added to increase pressure and complicate the environment. A well-positioned defender in the near-post zone, dealing only with the ball, is common in most defensive setups. Many times this is just enough pressure to put off the service to the box and affect the sight lines or timing of the runs. The addition of a defender to the near and far post requires a more accurate finish from the attackers. After reacquiring the sense of timing and delivery from both sides, introduce opponents to mark the runners. Start them off as a presence and gradually increase the resistance to full pressure. The action of the defending team is somewhat unpredictable, so encourage the attackers to improvise within reason and be creative with their choices. The players outside the box can still have a free go at goal but must make adjustments for the added traffic in front of them in order to get the ball on target. The runners need to stay alert and active until the play is over, and they may need to recycle the runs. Once a significant amount of success has been achieved, add an opponent to dispute the rebounded balls and help the clearance along. Finally, add enough opponents to create a counterattacking situation and organize the attacking team for countermeasures to maintain balance and safety.

Throw-In Near the Goal

Purpose

Improve the ability to attack directly to the goal or keep possession from a throw-in near the goal

Organization

Set up play on a standard field. Start with five players on the field, one player in position to throw the ball in play, and a defensive goal-keeper in goal.

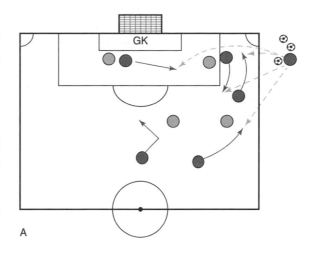

A

Procedure

1. See the starting positions of the players in diagram A.
2. Outline the actions of the principal players that will bring about the most direct scoring chance.
3. Create space around the thrower by taking up starting positions an adequate distance away from the ball.
4. The runners should feint actions at the start positions to gain a step on the opponents.
5. Determine a sequence of runs and the recycling of those runs if they are not an option to receive the ball.
6. Coordinate the goal scoring action (cross or shoot) with the rest of the players who will attack the goal.
7. Extra players are added to the activity at the discretion of the coach to apply pressure to the team in possession.

Once extra players are added, you can practice a specific near-the-goal throw-in play, such as the decoy run option (diagram B can serve as an example).

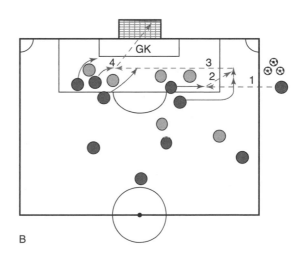

B

Key Points

- Throw the ball to feet and screen defenders when possible unless otherwise specified.
- Make sure to control the ball before the next action or give proper weight to the flick or one-touch pass.
- Instruct the thrower's reentry into the field of play after the pass.

Final Teaching Phase

In the final teaching phase, the organized tactical plans for corner kicks and throw-ins are trained and tested during free play. Two equal-sided teams play a game on an appropriately sized field at full speed. The coach may introduce conditions on the game to ensure many opportunities to execute corner kicks and throw-ins.

Half-Field Corner Kick—Throw-In Game

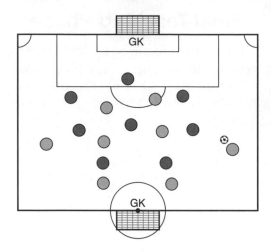

Purpose

Improving success of corner kicks and throw-ins during free play; practicing specifically for an upcoming match

Organization

Set up play on half of a standard field with a portable goal at the half line. There are two teams of nine players each, including goalkeepers, in a 1-3-3-2 or 1-2-4-2 formation.

Procedure

1. Play starts in the center of the field with a kickoff by a team.
2. Both teams have free play with some conditions and incentives.
3. The attacking team is awarded a corner kick after each goal it scores. The attacking team receives two corners if the defending team concedes a corner kick.
4. Goals scored from corner kicks or throw-ins have double value.
5. A team that successfully defends a corner kick is allowed 3 seconds of uncontested pressure in which to counterattack or keep possession.

Variation

Impose any rules or conditions that promote scoring from corners or throw-ins.

11

Direct and Indirect Free Kicks

Mark Berson

Set pieces are a critical part of the modern game of soccer. Interestingly, they occur more frequently in the biggest matches, where emotions run high and there's a tremendous amount of energy within the players on the field. For this reason, organization in both attack and defense in set pieces is important.

I sat in a stadium during a prestigious youth soccer tournament watching an American team play in the featured match against an international side. Around me were a number of college head coaches and assistants. A free-kick situation unfolded, during which the American team produced an excellent opportunity to score. A young assistant next to me said, "Hey, they just ran our SMU play—that's unbelievable." That was interesting to me, because this young man only knew part of the story. The head coach of the club team who had initiated the free kick had sent a player to the University of South Carolina (USC), where he played for us for 4 years. This player introduced the same set piece to us, and we adopted it. The young assistant's head coach was my assistant at the time, and he took the same set piece to his college. The young assistant had not just witnessed a team copying his set piece but rather had seen the original play in action. In such a way, set pieces are witnessed by coaches, embedded in their memory, and then reshaped and retooled in order to meet the demands of each particular team.

Attacking Free Kicks

The first order of business for the coach is to identify players within the team who may have special qualities enabling them to strike a ball accurately in a set-piece situation. One important quality to identify is the ability to bend a ball around or over a wall. Ideally, your team would feature a left-footed and a right-footed player with the same type of capabilities. Every effort should be made to identify these players and encourage them to further develop this set of skills. Repetition is critical here, and much of it will have to be carried out in individual work away from team training. Players should be encouraged to stay after training or come out on their own and work with the aid of an artificial wall and some goalkeepers in order to get the number of repetitions and quality of practice necessary to become proficient.

It is ideal to have a good right-footed and a good left-footed player involved in each free-kick situation over the ball. This creates an unsettled picture for the goalkeeper, who might expect a bending or dipping ball from either player, freezing him in position and preventing him from anticipating the flight of the ball.

Other specialists might include skilled headers of the ball, in many cases the center backs. They also need to spend extra time outside of team practice developing their timing and confidence in finishing chances that come to them.

Taking these concepts into consideration, we have developed a set-piece alignment at USC and used it successfully for many years, creating many variations of it. The setup allows for a balanced approach with many options. See figure 11.1 for an example of this alignment.

In this alignment, the space represented by the shaded area in the diagram is critical to the selection of the proper set piece. The closer the ball is positioned to the goal, the more important it is to get a shot or a one-touch-and-hit shot off. These options include the following.

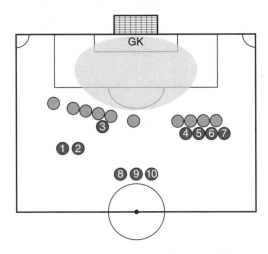

FIGURE 11.1   USC set-piece alignment.

Direct Shot

The first option is a direct shot by player 1 (right footed) or player 2 (left footed). See figure 11.2.

FIGURE 11.2 Direct shot by players 1 and 2.

Touch and Hit

The second option is a touch and hit by player 1 and player 2 working together. See figure 11.3.

FIGURE 11.3 Touch and hit by players 1 and 2.

Swerved Service

The next option is a swerved service by player 1 into players 4, 5, 6, and 7 for a direct header on goal. Player 3 spins around the wall in this option and positions for a ball headed back across the face of the goal. Because the goalkeeper will be pulled to the near post where the initial header should occur, the back-post area and player 3 may very well be open. See figure 11.4.

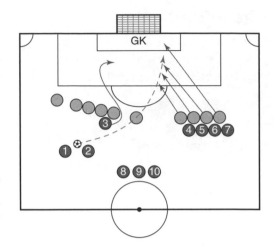

FIGURE 11.4   Swerved service by player 1.

Twin Towers

Another option is what we call the *twin towers*. In this option, player 2 and player 1 pretend to discuss their planned shot on goal. Player 2 moves away from the ball and player 1 moves up to apparently adjust the ball for his shot. In doing so, he places his toe under the ball and then lifts it over the wall to player 3, who has spun around the wall and into the space behind. Players 4, 5, 6, and 7 race into the attacking space for rebounds and to potentially finish up a ball that might be passed back across the face of the goal. Again, because the goalkeeper is pulled to the near post for the initial shot, the back-post area may well be open.

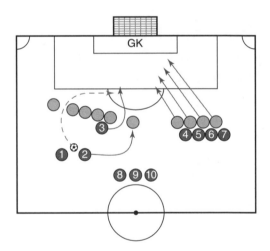

FIGURE 11.5   Twin towers by players 1 and 2.

SMU Play

A final option is the previously mentioned SMU play. Here player 2 runs over the ball to the outside of the wall. Player 1 plays the ball to the feet of player 4, who has run across laterally, gaining just a step on the marker. Player 4 plays a one-touch ball into the space behind the wall for player 2. Players 4, 5, 6, and 7 go to seal off the back post for a ball that may be slipped across to them. Again, the goalkeeper may be pulled to the near-post shot or pulled out to cut the angle of the onrushing

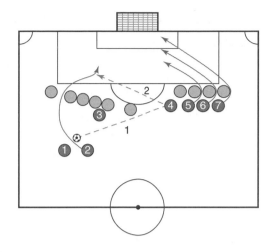

FIGURE 11.6 SMU play.

shooter and thus the back post may be wide open. See figure 11.6 for an example of the SMU play.

We use a number of hand signals to signify which of the attacking options we will execute in each set piece. This enables all of the players to anticipate the attacking movement and perhaps pull a defender into a less optimal position in each case. For instance, they may check away from the area that they need to run into and then cut back suddenly to free themselves of their marker. In another instance, they may distract the defenders from the ball, enabling a more opportunistic shot on goal.

In the attacking phase of our set pieces, we have the advantage of knowing exactly where the ball will go. We want to maximize that by dragging our opponents into the least favorable positions.

Direct and Indirect Kicks From Wide Positions

When direct and indirect kicks occur from wide positions, where a direct shot would not be advised, a number of options present themselves. One option would be to have two players standing over the ball with the abil-ity to serve the ball to the right or left. Player 1 might serve the ball to player 2, who has run over the ball to the outside of the wall. He then receives the ball in space and is able to cross it across the face of the goal to the target players 3, 4, 5, 6, and 7, who are attacking the goal. A second option would be for player 1 to play the ball square to player 3, who has checked across the face of the penalty area. He then plays a one-time ball behind the wall to player 2, who runs around the outside of the wall, receives the pass, and has the option to shoot or cross the ball (see figure 11.7).

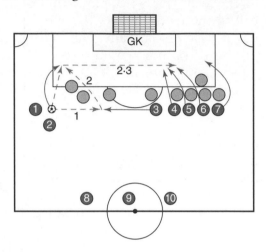

FIGURE 11.7   Penetrate the wall for a cross.

Another option would be a direct service curled into the attacking space inside the penalty area. This enables the onrushing players 4, 5, 6, and 7 to attack the ball in the space behind the wall. Again, careful consideration needs to go into the selection of players to serve these balls, and the players should be encouraged to spend extra time practicing this skill. See figure 11.8 for an example.

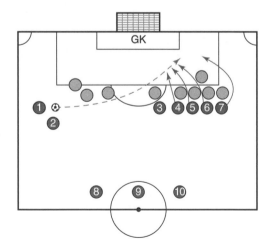

FIGURE 11.8   Indirect kick from wide service into targets.

Direct and Indirect Kicks From Deep Positions

The defending players in direct and indirect kicks from wide areas well outside the shooting area often hold attackers at the 18-yard (16 m) line.

In this instance it is sometimes advisable to run a player into the flank position (player 2) and then play the ball into the space where it can be served into the attacking zone. This enables players 3, 4, 5, 6, and 7 to break into attacking spaces inside the penalty area at a better angle to attack the cross. See figure 11.9 for an example.

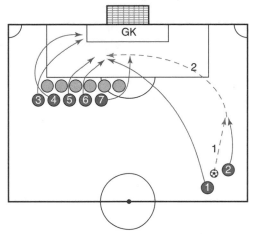

FIGURE 11.9   Play wide for a cross.

For indirect and direct kicks from central positions very deep, one option would be to quickly play the ball wide to a teammate. This enables the teammate to get into a wide position for a good service into the box. You will note that player 5 sets a pick for player 6 to run around to get into a favorable attacking position. See figure 11.10 for an example.

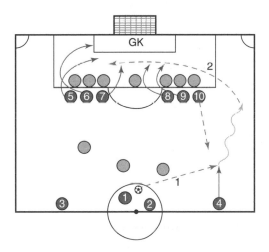

FIGURE 11.10   Indirect and direct kicks from central position.

Another option with free kicks from a deep central position is to line up the attacking players in wide positions at the 18-yard (16 m) line or wherever the defensive line holds them. The ball is then curled into the attacking space for one set of attacking players—either 5, 6, and 7 or 8, 9, and 10—who have run in one direction to lose their marks and then cut back sharply to receive the ball in space. The players receiving this ball initially may elect to head the ball on goal or head back across the face of the goal to the other set of attacking players. See figure 11.11 for an example.

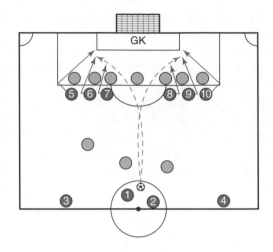

FIGURE 11.11 Left or right serve.

Indirect Kick Inside the Penalty Area

There is probably no more dramatic call in the world of indirect kicks than an indirect kick that's awarded inside the penalty area. In the most dra-

matic cases, the entire opposing team may line up on the goal line, with the goalkeeper in a position to quickly rush out and try to smother the kick. Two good options exist to attack this problem. The first is a ball played square from player 1 to player 2, who then chips the ball into the goal over the heads of the defenders. Another way to accomplish this objective is to have player 1 lift the ball with a foot and have player 2 volley the ball gently over the heads of the defenders. See figure 11.12 for an example.

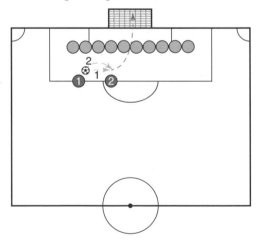

FIGURE 11.12   Indirect kick in the box.

Penalty Kicks

In their book *Soccernomics* (2009), authors Simon Kuper and Stefan Szymanski note that Basque economist Ignacio Palacio Huerta has recorded volumes of information on the way penalties are taken. His results are interesting to review as we look at the art of taking penalties.

Some of his findings are as follows:

- The team that goes first wins a penalty kick shootout 60 percent of the time.

- The number one quality of good penalty taking is unpredictability. This is for those players who take penalties on a regular basis and therefore are scouted and potentially charted by opponents.

- The optimal strategy to maximize scoring is for a penalty taker to kick 61.5 percent of the time to his natural side and 38.5 percent of the time to his other side.

- The goalkeeper's best strategy is to dive to the shooter's natural side 58 percent of the time and to the other side 42 percent of the time.

Kuper, S., and S. Szymanski. 2009. *Soccernomics: Why England loses, why Germany and Brazil win and why the U.S., Japan, Australia, Turkey and even Iraq are destined to become the kings of the world's most popular sport.* New York: Nation Books.

It is important to put this data into context. Certainly the scouting and recording of penalty takers and goalkeepers does occur at all levels of soccer competition. Therefore, it becomes important for your regular penalty-kick takers to be able to randomly change the spot to which they kick. For players selected for a tournament-deciding penalty-kick shootout, where no one was a regular penalty-kick taker during the course of the season and for whom no recorded data might exist, this might not be a critical factor. For those players, repetition focusing on one or two selected target areas for the penalty kick is an important point.

Training your selected players to score penalties is a challenge because the goalkeepers and penalty takers learn each other's tendencies in training. Though it is important for the goalkeeper to have training in facing penalties, it can also be a discouraging process for the goalkeeper to face multiple penalties from multiple players training for a penalty-kick shootout.

Taking into account many theories regarding penalties, I have used the following method to train penalty-kick takers. The pressure in the penalty-kick situation is on the shooter. We train our penalty takers to deal with the pressure that exists (hit the target with a quality strike) but not to create more pressure for them (guess which way the goalkeeper is going). Train to hit a spot with power and precision. Vary this only when you have been selected on multiple occasions to take kicks and you believe your data may have been inputted to the goalkeeper that you are against. When in doubt, keep it simple—place the ball down, avoid eye contact with the goalkeeper, and hit your target. The only poor penalty is one that misses the target. Because players do not know and cannot control the direction and timing of the goalkeeper's movement, they should only concentrate on hitting the target with precision and power.

We train penalties without a goalkeeper for many of the repetitions in the beginning. We use mannequins in the goal. This enables us to perform many repetitions of kicks and allows the kickers to repeatedly develop muscle memory in hitting the selected target on each kick. We then add a goalkeeper to the process to bring the entire event to game level. Our results are charted and posted (see figure 11.13 for an example). Players may elect to change their spot at any time. This also keeps the goalkeepers fresh and ready to vigorously defend penalties in the latter stages of training.

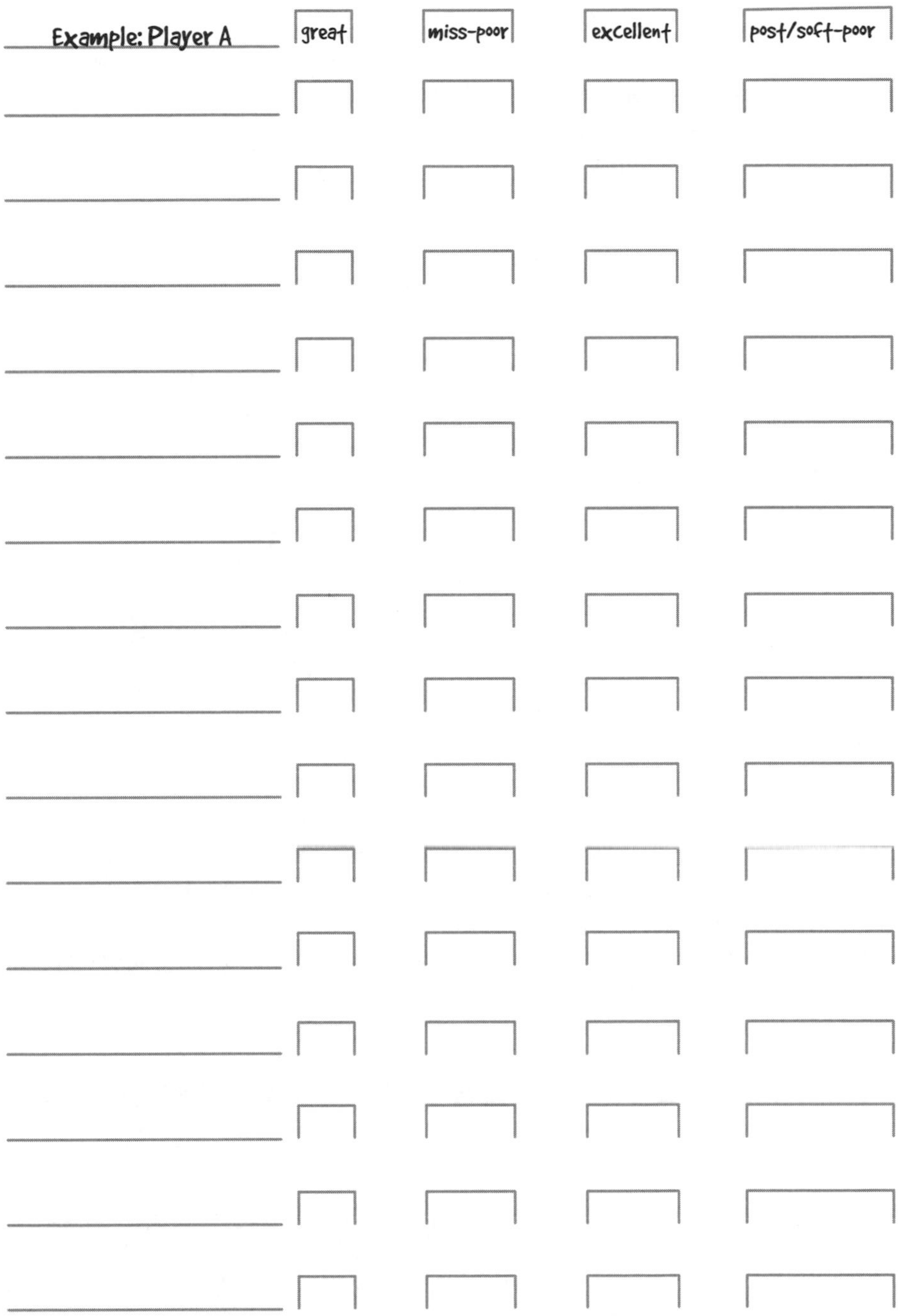

Example: Player A	great	miss-poor	excellent	post/soft-poor
_____	⌐¬	⌐¬	⌐¬	⌐¬
_____	⌐¬	⌐¬	⌐¬	⌐¬
_____	⌐¬	⌐¬	⌐¬	⌐¬
_____	⌐¬	⌐¬	⌐¬	⌐¬
_____	⌐¬	⌐¬	⌐¬	⌐¬
_____	⌐¬	⌐¬	⌐¬	⌐¬
_____	⌐¬	⌐¬	⌐¬	⌐¬
_____	⌐¬	⌐¬	⌐¬	⌐¬
_____	⌐¬	⌐¬	⌐¬	⌐¬
_____	⌐¬	⌐¬	⌐¬	⌐¬
_____	⌐¬	⌐¬	⌐¬	⌐¬
_____	⌐¬	⌐¬	⌐¬	⌐¬
_____	⌐¬	⌐¬	⌐¬	⌐¬
_____	⌐¬	⌐¬	⌐¬	⌐¬
_____	⌐¬	⌐¬	⌐¬	⌐¬

FIGURE 11.13 Penalty-kick data.

Training Options for Set Pieces

A team must have the ability to execute and defend set pieces under game-like conditions. However, training a set-piece organization for attacking and defending in a fun and fast-paced environment can be a challenge.

To do this, we train with two full teams on a half field with two goals. One goal is at the half line and one remains in its normal place at the end of the field. The field is approximately 60 yards (55 m) in length and the full width. Ideally, mannequins or artificial walls can be used to create the wall for each team. If not, we take the inside and outside rushers and one player who is marking man to man and use them to create a small three-man wall for the attackers to face. See figure 11.14 for the setup for this training.

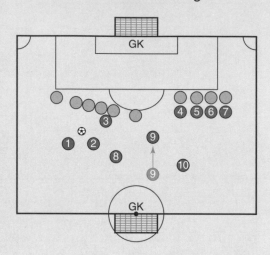

FIGURE 11.14   Half-field set-pieces training activity.

The teams are given time to rehearse and practice their options, and then they meet in a competition. The coaches have a chart to be sure that each team has an equal number of attacking opportunities from the right, left, and center at varying distances from goal.

This game can be scored a number of ways. We score as follows: 3 points for a goal, 1 point for a shot on goal saved by the keeper, and 1 point added to a goal scored on a counterattack. In this way, we increase our players' focus on both generating quick counterattacks and preventing counterattacks from set-piece situations.

Note that this drill can be modified for the early part of the season when more rehearsal is needed or for later in the season to prepare for an opponent's scouted strengths and weaknesses.

Attacking and defending from set-piece situations is a key component of today's game. With repetition in the skilled positions and a good understanding of the overall concepts of defending and attacking, your team can perform at a high level.

ABOUT THE EDITOR

Jay Miller's 40-year coaching career is the culmination of a life of competition and mentoring at every level of soccer. With a BS and MED in health and physical education from East Stroudsburg University, Jay began his career at Lebanon County High School, where he won the state championship, a first for the school. Later, coaching at the collegiate level, Jay led the University of Tampa to their first national title. As head coach for the University of South Florida, Jay won three conference titles.

Jay has served as a national teams coach and coaching instructor for the United States Soccer Federation since 1978. He has contributed to several technical reports for competitions, including the 1994 World Cup, 1996 Olympic Games, and the 1999 Women's World Cup. His international coaching includes qualifying the U-17 national team for the 1997 World Championships and serving as a national coach for the U-18, U-20, U-23, and full national teams. Coach Miller represented the U.S. State Department's Sports Envoy Program as an instructor and coach on tours to Morocco, Bolivia, and Thailand.

In 2012 Jay joined New England Revolution Professional Soccer Club as the first assistant. The following year the Revs returned to the MLS Playoffs after a four-year absence.

ABOUT THE CONTRIBUTORS

Jeff Pill (Individual Skills: Dribbling, Passing, and Receiving) served as the women's national staff coach for US Soccer and assistant coach for the U19 national team, posting an international record of 11-0-1. Since 1994 Pill has been part of the national instructional staff, helping to train the 1996 U.S. women's Olympic team and coordinating the U14 girls' national team program. Pill's 40-year career in soccer includes coaching at New Hampshire College and coaching high school soccer at the Derryfield School in New Hampshire. For seven consecutive years (1986-1992), the boys' team at Derryfield School won the

Jeff Pill

state championship. Under Pill's leadership, Derryfield's record included a 69-game winning streak and 122 games without being shut out. Pill coaches at Maranatha Baptist Bible College, the Midwest NCCAA regional champion in 2008. He is a professor in the sport management and physical education departments at Maranatha.

Ken Lolla (Attacking Through the Middle Third) is the head men's soccer coach at the University of Louisville and a former US Soccer midfielder. A collegiate coach for more than 20 years, Lolla has most recently guided Louisville in two consecutive Elite 8 appearances, an NCAA College Cup Final, and a number 1 national ranking. A two-time National Coach of the Year, coach Lolla and his staff have had 11 players drafted to Major League Soccer, the most of any program in the country. Lolla has served as the head coach for Akron University, Belmont University, and the U15 U.S. national team. A graduate of Duke

Ken Lolla

University, Lolla was a two-time All-American and went on to play professionally for several years. Ken is the author of *Finding Your Gifts*, a children's book that teaches life principles, and *Passing It On,* an educational manual for youth soccer coaches. Lolla is a frequent keynote speaker for businesses, sport teams, schools, and nonprofit organizations.

Thomas Durkin (Corner Kicks and Throw-Ins) has coached at every level from youth soccer to Major League Soccer and U.S. national teams. Currently the head coach for the Boston Breakers of the NWSL, Durkin most recently was with the Bradenton Academics (Premiere Development League) as general manager and head coach. He has led the Academics to more than 100 wins and the 2009 PDL national semifinals. He served as director of the IMG Soccer Academy, where he amassed over 300 wins and produced several professional players. He has two Dallas Cup Championships and two PDL Southeast Conference Championships to his name. His 2008-09 USSF Academy League team finished third in the nation.

Thomas Durkin

He has also been an assistant coach for both the U17 national team and the Tampa Bay Mutiny. Durkin has been an Olympic development program coach for both boys and girls and head coach at Richland College, Union College, and Rutgers University. He holds an "A" US Soccer Federation license, a FIFA Would Youth Football Academy diploma, an FAI Republic of Ireland coaching diploma, a KNVB international diploma, and a national staff coach instructor's badge.

Bobby Clark (Shooting and Finishing) is head coach of the men's soccer team at Notre Dame. He has guided his teams to 12 NCAA Championship appearances (including the 2013 NCAA Division I national title), two Big East tournament titles (2003 and 2012), and three Big East regular-season crowns (2004, 2007, and 2008). He was named 2013 ACC and NCAA Division I Coach of the Year.

Bobby Clark

Tony DiCicco (Goalkeeper in the Attack) is a soccer player, coach, and TV commentator. He is best known for coaching the U.S. women to an Olympic gold medal in 1996 and for winning the FIFA World Cup Championship in '99. In 2008 DiCicco coached the U.S. women's national team to victory in the FIFA U20 World Cup in Chile, making him the only U.S. coach to have won an Olympic gold medal and two FIFA World Cup Championships. DiCicco also was commissioner of the Women's United Soccer Association in 2000-2003. He served as a TV analyst for the ESPNs during the 2003, 2007, and 2011 Women's World Cup. DiCicco has also coached the Boston Breakers (Women's Professional Soccer League) from 2009 to 2011.

Tony DiCicco

Anson Dorrance (Team Possession) is the head coach of the women's soccer program at the University of North Carolina. He has one of the most successful coaching records in the history of sports. Under Dorrance's leadership, the Tar Heels have won 22 of the 33 national women's soccer championships since 1981. Under Dorrance, the Tar Heels have a .923 winning percentage over 35 seasons as of the conclusion of the 2013 season. He has led his team to a 101-game winning streak and coached 19 players who have won Collegiate National Player of the Year Awards. Fifty-two of his former and current Tar Heel players have earned caps with the U.S. women's national team. Dorrance has been recognized as National Coach of the Year in women's soccer seven times and as the Men's Soccer Coach of the Year in 1987. In 2008 Dorrance was inducted into the National Soccer Hall of Fame.

Anson Dorrance

Ian Barker (Specialty Skills: Crossing and Attack Heading) is the director of coaching education at the National Soccer Coaches Association of America (NSCAA). He joined the NSCAA staff after serving as the men's soccer coach at Macalester College in St. Paul, Minnesota, a position he assumed in 2003 after four years as an assistant coach for the squad. He was an assistant coach for the men's team at the University of Wisconsin from 1989 to 1997, helping the Badgers to four NCAA tournament appearances. The 1995 team won the Big Ten title and claimed the NCAA National Championship. He served as the state director of coaching and player development for the Minnesota Youth Soccer Association for 10 years. Barker currently serves as the head coach for Region II Boys ODP.

Ian Barker

John Hackworth (Creating Opportunities in the Attacking Third) is the interim manager of the Philadelphia Union. He helped guide the team to a first-place finish in group play in World Cup qualifying and a second-place finish in the 2009 FIFA Confederations Cup. He also served as technical director of the Development Academy, U.S. Soccer's player development initiative that launched in 2007. With the U.S. Under-17 Residency Program in Bradenton, Florida, Hackworth served as head coach of the 2005 and 2007 World Cup teams and an assistant coach of the 2003 World Cup team. In 2008 he earned the United States Olympic Committee Developmental Coach of the Year Award. He was head coach at the University of South Florida for four years and the top assistant at Wake Forest for five years. During his tenure at USF, he helped the Bulls to two NCAA Tournament appearances (1998 and 2001). In 1998, his squad won the Conference USA Tournament championship and a share of the C-USA regular-season title. For his efforts, he was named the league's Coach of the Year. While a student at Wake Forest, Hackworth played right back, helping his coach and Philadelphia soccer icon Walt Chyzowych lead the club to a third-place national ranking in 1991 and 1992. He played for the Carolina Dynamo of the A-League in 1997.

John Hackworth

Mark Berson (Direct and Indirect Free Kicks) has the most wins as an NCAA Division I head coach among active coaches and is ranked third among Division I head coaches with 455 victories. Berson has compiled 31 winning seasons in his 35 years at the University of South Carolina and made 20 appearances in the NCAA Men's Soccer Championship, including seven Sweet 16 appearances, four Elite 8s, two College Cup appearances, and one NCAA Championship final (1993). Since joining Conference USA in 2005, South Carolina won the conference tournament in 2005 and 2010 along with a regular-season championship in 2011.

Mark Berson

Berson has been a member of the US Soccer national instructional staff since 1989 and has served as coach of the U.S. men's U18 national team. University of South Carolina players have appeared for the U.S. men's national team in each of the last three FIFA World Cup finals (Josh Wolff, Clint Mathis, and Brad Guzan).

Mike Noonan (Attacking From the Defensive Third) is a retired American soccer player who played professionally in the American Indoor Soccer Association. He was a two-time NSCAA First-Team All-American at Middlebury College, where he graduated in 1983. He is currently the head coach of the Clemson University men's soccer team. Since his arrival at Clemson, he has led the Tigers to top 10 appearances in the national poll and has defeated several top 25 programs. He was head coach of the Wheaton College men's soccer team. The team had a 4-11-0 record his first season, but he took them to a 12-5-1 record his

Mike Noonan

second season. He coached at the University of New Hampshire from 1991 to 1994 and led the Wildcats to their first NCAA Tournament appearance. In 1995 he became head coach of the Brown University men's soccer team. Noonan's teams earned 8 Ivy League titles and 10 NCAA postseason tournament appearances in 15 seasons with the Bears. In 2013 at Clemson he won his 250th career match during his 25th year of coaching. Noonan was inducted into the Connecticut Soccer Hall of Fame in 2011.

Dean Wurzberger (Attacking From the Flanks) has been involved in state and national coaching education and licensing programs for US Soccer since 1988. Before joining the coaching staff of Andromeda FC, he was a player scout and team evaluator for the US Soccer Development Academy in the Dallas–Fort Worth area. As a US Soccer staff instructor, Wurzberger tutors and assesses men's and women's coaches at the youth, high school, collegiate, and professional levels throughout the United States. Before relocating to the Dallas area in 2011, Wurzberger spent 19 years leading the University of Washington men's soccer program, becoming the program's all-time winningest coach. Wurzberger holds the English FA UEFA "A" coaching license.

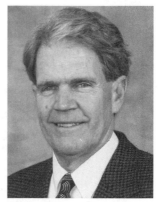

Dean Wurzberger